Weekly Masonic Doubts

A pocket companion of squarely critical ponderings for the 21st century

ISTVÁN HORVÁTH

First published by Cravat Books 2023.
Hamilton, Canada.

Copyright © 2023 by István Horváth

All rights reserved. No part of this publication may be reproduced, stored or transmitted in any form or by any means, electronic, mechanical, photocopying, recording, scanning, or otherwise, without written permission from the publisher. It is illegal to copy this book, post it to a website, or distribute it by any other means without permission.

Foreword by David J. Cameron
Cover by the author using a drawing from the book *Studium universalis* by Valentin Weigel (1533-1588).

Social Science / Freemasonry & Secret Societies

István Horváth has no responsibility for the persistence or accuracy of URLs for external or third-party internet websites referred to in this publication and does not guarantee that any content on such websites is, or will remain, accurate or appropriate.

Disclaimer.
All the opinions are solely of the author, and they do not represent the official view of any of the Lodges, Grand Lodges, and other Masonic bodies and are not intended to be seen as such.

First edition
ISBN: 978-0-9919845-2-7 paperback
ISBN: 978-0-9919845-3-4 hard cover
ISBN: 978-0-9919845-1-0 e-book

To Tanja, for her patience, and for welcoming all the Masonic stories in our lives

The matter whereof SOLOMONS Temple was built, was of three sorts, stones, wood, and metals [...] The matter of wisedomes Temple shall be supplyed out of the store of three sorts of principles, Sense, Reason, and divine Revelation.

Comenius, 1642

Let Masonry use the pen and the printing-press in the free State against the Demagogue; in the Despotism against the Tyrant.

Albert Pike

CONTENTS

Foreword — xi
Preface — xiii
Acknowledgements — xv
1 Morals and politics — 1
2 On landmarks — 3
3 The prime lessons of the prime numbers — 6
4 Why is Freemasonry so fragmented? — 9
5 What is brotherly love? — 11
6 Why do we need God? — 13
7 What if no union in 1813? — 15
8 Antients and Moderns - Schism No. 1 — 17
9 One day Masons… — 20
10 On forget-me-not — 21
11 What is Freemasonry and what I am doing in it? — 23
12 History and beginnings — 25
13 Prince Hall - Schism No. 2 — 27
14 On origins — 29
15 Organizations of Masons in the past? — 31
16 Mysticism and history — 33

17 On time	36
18 Grand Orient of France – Schism No. 3	38
19 Why Initiation?	41
20 Everybody was a Mason…	43
21 Discrimination and judgment	44
22 Founding fathers and brewers	46
23 Can women be Freemasons?	48
24 On elite(s)	51
25 Freemasons in the Bible	53
26 Deviation	55
27 On secrecy	57
28 The shame	59
29 On ritual	61
30 Freethinkers or conformists	63
31 On music	66
32 Internal versus external	69
33 How many is too many	71
34 On Masonic philosophy	74
35 The double heritage	77
36 On heroes & education	79
37 Admonitions of Szent István	82
38 Concerning God and Religion - today	86

39 Is this a theatre play?	*89*
40 Democracy incubators?	*92*
41 The Temple in the air	*95*
42 The linguistic analysis that never happened	*100*
43 The missed symbolism	*104*
44 On spirituality	*107*
45 Whose symbol it is anyway?	*109*
46 Favourite seven at the festive board	*113*
47 Inheriting the heritage	*119*
48 The Templars: legends and more legends	*122*
49 Barn raising or bar raising	*125*
50 Lodges and lodges	*127*
51 Mystery plays and the Hiramic legend	*129*
52 What about your soul?	*133*
Epilogue (bonus chapter)	*136*
About the author	*141*
Bibliography	*143*

x

FOREWORD

Freemasonry is the largest and oldest fraternity in the world, but it is hidden under a veil of misguided secrecy. There is much about the fraternity that even its members do not know. Its history is obfuscated by many manufactured origin myths, but it certainly has existed from the 16th century, and was first organized into national bodies in the 18th. Masons meet to act out ancient morality plays, for their own edification and for that of their new initiates, along the way involving themselves in other aspects of improving the human condition for all people.

It may seem like a monolithic organization that is unchanging, but the reality is that it has taken many forms at different times and in different places. While [almost] always dedicated to self-improvement, it has expressed this in a multitude of ways, from esoteric meditation to community charity, and even to political involvement. Unless one travels widely, one often thinks that all Masons do exactly what the brethren in one's own district do. And that we do the same things now as we did since time immemorial. Neither is the case.

Worshipful Brother Horváth grew up in Transylvania, an area of the world that has historically been part of several kingdoms, countries, and empires, and therefore has been exposed to many ways of being. He worked as a teacher, a journalist, and a translator. Fluent in four languages, he brings to the study of Freemasonry, a curiosity about the language used, and what the brethren of the past understood by it. And he challenges us to think about our ritual and what it means – in terms of our practice, our polity, and our philosophy.

Brother Horváth was initiated in Freemasonry in the "regular and perfect lodge Egyenlőség" (=Equality), under the Symbolic Grand Lodge of Hungary. In Ontario, Canada, he affiliated with the Electric Lodge, serving as Worshipful Master from 2018 to 2022. He is also a founding member of Templum Lucis Lodge, the second Observant Lodge formed in Ontario. Observant lodges strive to give candidates and members an impactful experience by promoting excellent ritual, frequent and in-depth education, and a full festive board.

One of my mentors, M.W. Bro. Raymond S. J. Daniels, used to say, "As free-thinking or Speculative Masons, I cannot tell you *how* to think, nor can I tell you *what* to think, but hopefully I can give you something to *think* about." In this provocative little book, W. Bro. Horváth has also accomplished that worthy goal.

David J. Cameron
Past Grand Master
The Grand Lodge of Canada in the Province of Ontario

PREFACE

It is important to approach this book and its weekly thoughts offered to the reader as a very private mental exercise: just you, the reader, and your thoughts looking into your soul. Otherwise, the whole idea is in vain. The author hopes that each week focusing on one single topic or idea or fact… would help you to clear your mind and contemplate what that week's topic means for the reader.

This exercise is a lonely activity, akin to meditation when your soul and mind are connected with the Universe. We can and should be as sincere with ourselves as possible. Cheating ourselves is not worthy of a Mason. For some questions, the reader might already have an answer or be able to find one easily. For some other topics, the reader may need a week to contemplate before arriving at a conclusion.

Although – and this is extremely important – nobody is giving you a task, like you had to prepare your homework in school. You don't have to come up with an "answer". Just as we say about Freemasonry: the important thing is the journey, the road we travel mentally in order to explore our inner self. Look into the "inner chamber" of your mind and heart! That's where your answers are…

Even if we don't admit it publicly, confronting our own ideas, fears, and doubts could be the most difficult enterprise in the world. Just as is questioning our own dominant convictions that we've considered as a "given" for a long time. Try to read this book with an open but questioning mind: you can agree with the ideas in it, or you may even feel outrage if it contradicts your opinions. The important thing is to ponder what you read and add your own thoughts.

As practical advice, it is suggested that you read one chapter, and think about it during the following days and, after a week, read another part. And the next week, another one... Of course, one can just sit down on a quiet afternoon or a long evening and read the entire book in one sitting. But even if you do that, it is worth returning to the individual chapters, one at a time, as a daily advancement.

With brotherly love to my fellow Masons and everyone else interested in learning more.

The author

The author acknowledges that their home is located on/in territoire traditionnel des peuples Anishinaabeg, Haudenosaunee, Attiwonderonk et de la Première nation des Mississaugas du Crédit. Ce territoire est couvert par le Traité 3. Today, this place is still the home to many Indigenous people from across Turtle Island and we are grateful to have the opportunity to work, live, and play together on this land.

ACKNOWLEDGEMENTS

I am grateful to all those Masonic and non-Masonic authors who published so many thought-provoking writings that inspired my humble attempt to offer a small practical guidebook to my brothers to serve as a companion for their daily advancement and weekly contemplations.

Many people, Masons, and non-Masons, did read my manuscript in making and provided extremely useful feedback and valuable suggestions. **Stefan Streitferdt** was the first to read the articles as drafts, and I am grateful for his insights and patient help, and the very much needed corrections. **Joel Simkin** reviewed the language, and I am thankful for his delicate approach and balancing to keep my unusual style yet make it palatable for the readers.

The **Virtual Order of Sapere Aude** (*VOOSA*) and its host, **David Chichinadze**, were instrumental in pushing me to write several presentations for their international audience, and the comments of my educated brothers inspired more articles and encouraged me to continue the work. A planned project with **Duncan Burden** planted the seed for many topics discussed in this book.

Among the first readers of the draft were also: Milan Čobanov, Edward F. Dunsmore, Dale Graham, Allison Growling, Mark Kikot, Matthew Maennling, Obinna Onyewuchi, John Raso, Tom Wills, Aaron Smith, Michael Wood, (Ontario), Taylor Nauta (Louisiana), Josef

Schreiner, Mark Walton (Hungary), Alan D. Rudland (Scotland), Cameron M. Bailey (Washington), Matthew Shelton (Michigan), and their time and feedback have provided invaluable contributions towards the manuscript's improvement, and I extend my thanks. The author of the Foreword, **David J. Cameron**, not only was among the first readers but volunteered to help making this book better.

Before I even dared to think about writing a book on this continent, two members of my first Canadian lodge—Electric No.495, the stepmother lodge—Peter Mouriopoulos and William (Bill) Millar mentored me in learning how the Craft operates on this continent, and they also read, years ago, my very first attempt at a Masonic essay, providing great feedback and encouragement, and those times were not forgotten.

I am worried that I missed acknowledging everyone who supported me to get to where I am now. With due apologies, I feel grateful for the time we spent together, for the stimulating discussions, and sharing thoughts.

Cover Image Credits

The book cover image is originally from the book **Studium universalis** by *Valentin Weigel* (1533-1588) and has been copied and coloured many times over the centuries. Weigel was a village preacher, but secretly wrote spiritual texts that were not published until after his death. Although the authorities banned his writings, their influence was far-reaching.

The three large spheres refer to the concept of 'three principles' in the cosmos - light, darkness, and nature. The 'tree of the soul' is also depicted, according to this idea, our "tree of the soul" can blossom and produce good "fruits" only by divine help (the hand reaching from heaven).

Weekly Masonic Doubts

The version of the original drawing by
Valentin Weigel used for the cover

1 MORALS AND POLITICS

Masons often speak from their high horse of their perceived *moral* superiority as Craft members – yet carefully avoid voicing their opposition to governments that commit *immoral* acts.

How far can the "ban" go (regarding the discussion of *politicks* and religion) in the lodge – and beyond – to suppress the moral obligation of every human being, especially ethical men, of standing up for those values they confess to cherish and honour?

While certainly the transformation of Masonic lodges into political debate clubs or similar institutions is not preferred (it's one of those axioms that never get questioned, but accepted, allegedly from time immemorial…), the larger issue of civic duties rarely is considered. The conflict between what we could call the internal moral standards, and the imposed rules of behaviour, putting external ethical limits on the expression of internal moral values – doesn't seem to clash in our institution. We look at it as something natural or given – nothing there to question.

We developed the comfortable stance that we let courts, judges, or politicians define what is, or should be, considered the "correct" way to behave, speak, and think; and somehow, in a mysterious way, we attempt to internalize it as a moral guide, which from that point on cannot be questioned or challenged, since that would go against the accepted framework of the discourse in the public sphere.

Masons promise to be law-abiding citizens (subjects, for monarchists) of the land and to obey the government. They also promise to adhere to the noble ideals and moral values they learn and teach in the lodges. We must really think the world is an ideal place – since the possibility of conflicts between obedience and sticking to internal norms never comes up in our discussions.

2 ON LANDMARKS

The Book of Constitution of my present jurisdiction (Grand Lodge of A.F.&A.M. of Canada in the Province of Ontario) refers to the "Landmarks" in three places in its text: page 29 twice; p. 136 once. Yet, there is not (nor has there ever been) a published list of the "Ancient Landmarks" that our Grand Lodge would consider the ultimate and definitive list. In plain English, the Grand Lodge of Ontario doesn't have a "list of landmarks" even if we acknowledge their existence and we refer to them.

Incidentally, the *Book of Constitutions – Craft Rules* of the United Grand Lodge of England (UGLE) does not contain a list of said landmarks either, even though it mentions them (the Antient) Landmarks seven [7] times. Only the requirement of belief in a Supreme Being is expressly mentioned as an "essential Landmark of the Order".

Should we assume that these two Grand Lodges don't respect the Antient Landmarks because they didn't list them in a document? Since we are discussing an institution with well-known English (British) roots, it may seem obvious to draw parallels between the unwritten (uncodified) character of the English constitution and their unwritten Antient Landmarks. Or would that be too big a stretch? I don't think so. Legal systems may differ considerably, and the lack or existence of a certain type of documents is due to historical developments, and don't presume superiority or inferiority. Any Canadian resident can witness this daily: besides the provinces (equivalent of states elsewhere) using the English type of Common Law, we also have Québec with its own legislation based on the *Code Napoléon*.

As a side note, though related: even the Basic Principles for recognition of foreign grand lodges have been "written" and were published only in 1929, never before. (They have been modified since then, at least on two occasions… that much for the commonplace "from time immemorial".)

Albert Mackey was an educated, intelligent man, a benevolent graphomaniac. But a graphomaniac, nonetheless. He wrote a lot, and at that time his works were considered the best by the standards of that era. But that was more than one and a half centuries ago! We should review his entire Masonic literature and analyze it by comparing it to the latest research. Unfortunately, too often he is revered with a total lack of criticism, and his opinions quoted with the medieval mantra: *"magister dixit"* [1]. Attempts to revise his widely accepted assumptions are heavily resisted by the general Masonic population.

Mackey is also a product of his land. American Masonry developed in ways that differ from Masonry in England, or even in Canada, and as Henry W. Coil describes it so fittingly, during the 19th century it became extremely focused on legislating itself with ideas borrowed from the civil and criminal law of the emerging American states. Nowhere else in the world did Freemasonry become so "legislated", i.e. regulated as in the jurisdictions of the USA. Even today we have – internationally – several

---

[1] Latin: the master said so.

"rules" like the American doctrine of "one land, one grand lodge". A convenient tool to make the Prince Hall lodges "irregular"…

In the fervent era of the 19th century, American Freemasonry produced a large number of authors of impressive tomes and works. However, we must keep in mind that in the past 50-60 years or so, an abundant body of new research emerged, documents have resurfaced and have been published, new interpretations developed, and academia finally started to study our Craft with the professional interest it deserves.

In spite of all these developments, there is still a strong tendency among Masons to quote and refer to only 19th century "dusty" authors, as if time stopped there for them. Most of the time, just pointing to Mackey's 25 landmarks immediately provokes the debate: because Oliver listed 40 landmarks, Pound 7, West Virginia 7, New Jersey 10, Nevada 39, and Kentucky 54. Other bodies have a shorter or longer list…

The data in the previous paragraph demonstrate that no Masonic jurisdiction can be judged by the number of codified landmarks in their documents.

Most of those rules should pertain to the so-called regularity of the Masonic bodies – lodges and, especially, Grand Lodges – rather than to the individual Mason's moral uprightness. Because no matter how many rules and regulations we codify in a "constitution", the quality of Freemasonry in any given jurisdiction will depend on how much those external rules are interiorized by each member. True, it is difficult to "measure". Maybe that's why nobody wants to talk about it. Instead, we compose and list rules, and we focus on the adherence to the letter of those rules, while having difficulty understanding and living by the spirit of Masonic "law".

3 THE PRIME LESSONS OF THE PRIME NUMBERS

We all learn in school what the prime numbers are. And then we immediately forget it – unless mathematics becomes our field of work. Later, some of us become Masons, so we have another encounter with those strange (natural) numbers that cannot be divided by anything else but 1 and themselves. 2 is also a prime number, although nobody pays attention to it. And the following prime numbers in sequence are 3, 5, 7…

Every Mason is familiar with those numbers – they are omnipresent in our rituals and allegorical stories that are used to teach us ethical lessons. There is even a nasty joke stating that Freemasons do everything three times to which the young wife concludes with disappointment that her husband is not a Mason. As it happens with many words, ideas, and elements of our rituals, we are prone to think that they are "masonic inventions", and we are shocked when we discover that they are used by many other people as well.

Looking back on the intellectual history of mankind, it seems obvious that as soon as our ancestors figured out how to count, the fascination with prime numbers started. And beginning with the early mythical oral traditions, these numbers took a central place in our stories. They are found in pagan myths, in the biblical narrative, and also in fairy tales and popular legends. Three goddesses competed for the golden apple (of discord) in Greek mythology; Snow White met with seven dwarfs; King Lear had three daughters, and we all have five fingers on each of our hands, we say hip, hip, hooray three times… In my childhood's fairy tales, the dragon always had seven heads. And there were three little pigs.

Even our modern "mythology" created mainly by Hollywood, is full of titles like *The Magnificent Seven* (or its inspiration, *The Seven Samurai*) and *Seven Brides for Seven Brothers*… and we could continue with *The Three Musketeers* and *The Three Days of the Condor*.

For those that have been socialized and educated in Western culture, the notion of the seven mortal sins should also be familiar. And when we are told about the three, five, seven (or more) steps, we are also taught that three rule a lodge, five hold a lodge, and seven make it perfect! Which raises the question: are the seven mortal sins perfect? While it seems to be a *contradictio in sine*, the question isn't without any merit. In the framework of hamartiology – the theological discipline studying sin – the seven sins could very well be perfect.

Our Craft is not a lonely, isolated entity hanging out there in the vacuum on a cable tow… it is a cultural and social product of its time, deeply embedded in universal human condition and knowledge. All we need to do is to place our Craft in the proper context, to view it in its relations to other important aspects of our culture. It is not special or unique because of its origins. It is special and unique because of its aims.

Prime numbers are everywhere. But only Freemasonry built a peculiar system on them to convey moral lessons in beautiful stories. Let's think about the stories that we should tell our newest followers: three, five, seven… or more.

4 WHY IS FREEMASONRY SO FRAGMENTED?

Yes, we all have a simple, "obvious" answer but let's put that aside and investigate it from a different angle.

In name and declarations, we are the most "universal" fraternity on the Earth. Brotherhood, tolerance, love – we throw those slogans around daily, without ever thinking about them. Even more, individually, we like to state things like "for me every Mason is a brother, no matter…" and here you can add your favourite part. Yet, we tend to forget that individual Freemasons or lodges don't have the ability to decide whom they regard as legitimate Masons. Only Grand Lodges have the authority to declare the regularity of another body and to initiate and maintain amical relations with it. It's like with the diplomatic relationships between countries: one may like a particular distant new country but only the government of our own country can establish official "mutual recognition". Of course, the lack of this recognition can cause hardship in travelling or trade, but the parallel existence still remains a fact, and the citizens of that unrecognized nation are still members of humankind.

We all are familiar with those (in)famous lists issued from time to time by our own grand body from which we learn the foreign grand bodies accepted as regular good guys by our own governing authority. Let's imagine for a moment a different list, a list that would have all the Grand Lodges and Grand Orients that are *not* recognized by your own grand lodge. Without any further notes or comments regarding the reasons for the lack of amity. Just (as in the existing list) the name of the grand body to which we don't extend the proverbial Masonic 'brotherly love'. The unbrotherly list.

Excepting the obvious con men and their "bogus" organizations created for personal commercial gains (about which bodies we are going to reflect another day, another week) the lack of recognition is, usually, based on formalistic and/or legalistic motives. And we are becoming more and more rigid in our interpretations of "true Freemasonry" – losing exactly the distinctive character of universal freethinkers. It is becoming akin to the religious wars: just because our fellow human worships the same deity in a different manner, we are going to war against him to impose our own "true" way of thinking.

A last thought. The tenets and principles of our Craft are the results of centuries old historical changes and development. Today they seem to be static, immovable, if you will, but we don't know what the future is holding for us.

Ponder over that unbrotherly list.

5 WHAT IS BROTHERLY LOVE?

In Masonic circles *politically correct* is disguised as "brotherly love". But the idea is the same: don't offend the poor man, even if he is wilfully ignorant and talks nonsense standing high on a soap box.

If you do speak up – you are not showing proper brotherly love toward that poor brother, who still tries his best to put together two sentences. One can observe this reproach many times in different Masonic forums and groups.

The notion of "politically correct" is, in general, a completely wrong idea: it just fuels the "offended culture". Everybody is offended by something... So, in order to avoid offending – we try to castrate the language, we try to invent non-existent pronouns, we invent strange phrases (Caucasian, Afro-American), and we use euphemisms[2] as avoidance.

Was the original "brotherly love" really meant to suppress the honest opinion and discussion? Or did it refer to something else that we don't understand today? How

---

[2] Euphemism – a word used to replace another word that is considered inadequate or offensive

can Masons have a healthy debate confronting ideas and opinions if we are not sincere, and if we are not naming things and notions correctly? Not "politically" correctly but grammatically correctly – just think of the seven liberal arts and sciences, especially the Trivium, the language related disciplines: Grammar, Rhetoric, Logic.

(What about Truth? Nobody remembers that… we only quote the Brotherly Love when we want to be offended. And we feel Relief whenever the honest man is intimidated by the ignorami.)

Does anyone know what brotherly love means, where it comes from (as a bad translation) and what the original intent of the meaning was? I will wait, go look it up!

There were five different words for LOVE used by ancient Greeks – only one can be translated as "brotherly love". And even when we do, we need an adjective to qualify it, since English is poorer here than ancient Greek: it is impossible to express the same concept with only one single word. The one word we have is too much and too little at the same time.

William Penn named the city Philadelphia, which is Greek for "brotherly love," derived from the Ancient Greek terms φίλος *phílos* (beloved, dear) and ἀδελφός *adelphós* (brother, brotherly).

6 WHY DO WE NEED GOD?

We are not going to question anybody's personal faith or belief system or what is colloquially called religion – the idea is to contemplate the role, necessity if you will, of the GAOTU in the regular Anglo-American Freemasonry. Yes, that's a mouthful – the thoughts in this one sentence might be enough for weeks of contemplation and pondering.

However, we should focus on the formal requirement in the regular Craft: an applicant must believe in a Supreme Being. It is up to our own conscience whether we see this requirement as a good thing or something else. Let's leave that for another occasion. For this week's question is: – why we need this requirement? Or, to put it more bluntly: why do we need God in Freemasonry.

Certainly, we have all heard many arguments trying to prove or explain the necessity of such a basic requirement, which is also one of the Basic Principles (1929) that form the rules for recognition of Grand Lodges. Some say it is the tradition and our proverbial respect for it. Maybe, but there was a time when getting completely drunk during and after the monthly meetings was also part of the "tradition" and it didn't survive. Which implies that not all traditions are good. Or are they?

And then there is the ubiquitous explanation that taking the Obligation without faith in a Supreme Being would "invalidate" it because – and this is the worrisome part – without fearing God's punishment we would not honour our solemn oath. For a fraternity boasting the highest moral values and often referring to the fact that a Mason's handshake is as strong as a written contract... the argument sounds weak. Some say, just plain wrong.

Let's take a closer look. If a Mason is good, i.e., behaves as a good man only because he fears that the Supreme Being punishes vice and rewards virtue, then, perhaps, he is not the good man we thought he was. A good man is a good man is a good man. And the cliché says that he must be a good man – even before we initiated him. However, if that's true, and he is a good man, then it follows that there is no need for a Supreme Law Enforcer to make him keep his solemn obligation. Some believe we need the divine force to keep us in line.

[There is a danger of a rabbit hole here: the moral dilemma has been present since the ancient Greek philosophers, known as the Euthyphro dilemma, in one of Plato's dialogues. And it continues to challenge philosophers and theologians of all persuasions – this is just a pointer for those who would like to read more.] In our case it should be a simple question, although not completely without theological and philosophical resonances. Incidentally, all the deeper contemplations, including our weekly mental exercise, do have philosophical – maybe even theological – implications. We rarely discuss them, unfortunately, but we should. In ancient times they considered philosophy a "guide" to live a meaningful life. Wisdom. Love of wisdom[3]. There is nothing wrong with loving it, even if we just aspire to have it... Back to our opening question: why do we need God in Freemasonry?

---

[3] Philo+Sophia, literally: love of wisdom.

7 WHAT IF NO UNION IN 1813?

We would have a Masonry without the hegemony of UGLE (United Grand Lodge of England).

We know very well that "what if…" type of questions are ahistorical and useless – yet, sometimes it's unavoidable to think about a small(?) fact in Masonic history: what if the (in)famous Union of the Moderns and Antients had not happened in 1813, in England?[4]

The last time it came to my mind was when browsing (for unrelated reasons) the document titled Aims and Relations of the Craft. The first time it was made public in 1938 by the UGLE and the other two "Home Grand Lodges" [Scotland and Ireland] – changing just the references to include their own name. And then, after the

---

[4] The Premier Grand Lodge of England (initially, only of London and Westminster) was organized in 1717; in 1751 a rival Grand Lodge, labeled the "Antient" was started. They called the London Grand Lodge "Modern" referring to the innovations introduced by this body. The two competing grand lodges existed until 1813, when after long negotiations a compromise was reached, and the creation of a new, "united" grand lodge ended the hostilities.

WWII, it was re-issued in 1949, stating that *nothing has changed that would warrant a modification of the document.*

Except that about 50 million people died... but we don't talk politics!

The rest is the usual formulas that we already knew since 1929 (The Basic Principles, modified in 1982) and from the 1938 original. Nothing even worth mentioning... except the tone of the last sentence:

They [the aims explained in the document] *"must be accepted and practised wholeheartedly and in their entirety by those who desire to be recognised as Freemasons by the United Grand Lodge of England"*.

Two questions, without sounding heretical or who-knows-what.

What if one day all the Grand Lodges around the world withdrew the recognition from the UGLE... leaving them alone in their pompous imperial British solitude?

What if the Union never happened and English Freemasonry weren't the monolithic and narrowminded formalized institution that it is today... but a diverse, multifaceted and decentralized loose association of lodges?

I know it is not Masonic, but I beg you for a moment to think —

Without the Union of 1813 there would be more than one Grand Lodge in England, and no Masonic body would be able to impose their view on the rest of the world. Let's make it clear: it doesn't really matter whether they are right or wrong – the issue is the attitude, the (arrogant) entitlement that they can dictate to the whole world.

Go on! Imagine what the global Masonic landscape would look like – without the unchallenged hegemony of the United Grand Lodge of England and the bunch of Grand Lodges self-titled as "regular"!

8 ANTIENTS AND MODERNS - SCHISM NO. 1

We, in the *regular* Anglo-American Freemasonry, are inclined to think about the Craft as a monolith uniform fraternity, that must be practised everywhere exactly as we do in our own little village lodge. Of course, the truth is far from that belief.

It is not true today and it wasn't true even 250 years ago. Diligent students of our history know that at that time there were two competing Grand Lodges in England. Scholars would mention here that there were, actually, three Grand Lodges, but this third one in York, disappeared soon...

The lasting rivalry was between the Premier Grand Lodge (of London and Westminster) founded in 1717 and the so-called "Antients" started in 1751. The Masons in the latter one nicknamed those in the former as "Moderns" – a reference to the alleged changes and innovations committed by the Premier Grand Lodge. In the English-speaking Freemasonry the term *schism* refers to this rivalry between the Antient and Modern Grand Lodges during the second half of the 18th century, until the well known compromise and union of 1813, when they merged and UGLE (hence the word "united" in the United Grand Lodge of England) was born.

There is even a book with this title – *Schism*[5] –, written by a prominent Masonic scholar and historian. However, in the official narrative of the UGLE they are very shy about this episode in the history of English Freemasonry. Browsing their website one would never guess that the present governing body that claims unwritten primacy over the whole world's Masonry, has been seriously challenged by the competing Grand Lodge for six decades... Moreover, the two other grand lodges in the British Isles, the Grand Lodge of Ireland and the Grand Lodge of Scotland recognized as "regular", i.e. true and proper Masonic body, the Antient Grand Lodge during this schism. (Together those three are known today as the Home Grand Lodges.)

The reasons for the schism were many. Not only Masonic considerations, as changes in ritual, knocks, passwords, arrangements of the lodge room etc. but also social and economical. The book referenced above gives an excellent overview of the events. For our weekly contemplation it is worth remembering that for a long time Freemasonry was a live and flexible organization, changing and morphing itself according to the requirements of the era. It was only in the past hundred years or so that it's got frozen in a rigid anachronistic posture.

An interesting fact: As Freemasonry started to spread across the English Channel towards Europe and across the Atlantic to the British colonies of North America, all the above mentioned Grand Lodges from the British Isles chartered lodges, providing them with the rules and ceremonial rituals of that peculiar moment in time. And those lodges (that later organized themselves in new

---

[5] Berman, Ric. *Schism*. Liverpool University Press, 2013.

territorial Grand Lodges) preserved rituals, knocks, ceremonies, furniture as they "borrowed" from their contemporaries… and later never changed. They are often like time capsules, reminding the students of Masonry of bygone eras.

It would be an interesting research to learn where did your Grand Lodge originate from and when…

And a final thought: this was the only schism in the history of the Craft that has been restored and reconciled.

9 ONE DAY MASONS...

According to the statistics the retention rate among one-day Masons and the traditional progression through the degrees, including the initiation and its alleged deep experience... are very similar, which creates an evergreen dilemma.

What does this say about the quality of the ritual that is supposed to convey and create the initiatic experience which must be unique and lasting for a lifetime?

Obviously, in most cases the ritual and the experience offered through it are not that great, evidently not greater or more impressive than the 'theatrical display' of the degree work (similar to how in the AASR - Scottish Rite - happens in most places) presented in the one-day events.

Personally, I'd like to see ritual work in our lodges that makes such a profound impression on the candidates that they will never consider leaving the Craft.

Why do initiates leave your lodge?

10 ON FORGET-ME-NOT

There is a story about this small blue flower – the forget-me-not – which is often quoted by Masons: allegedly, during the dark Nazi era in Germany, before WWII, when the regime outlawed Freemasonry in the 1930s, instead of the "usual" square and compasses pin, the members of the Craft started to wear a small forget-me-not flower lapel pin. And because of this historical event, we have even today such pins, since they became a cherished reminder of our belonging.

Wonderful story – too bad it is not true.

The myth has been debunked by many serious scholarly publications and by internationally renowned Masonic (and non-Masonic) authors. Most of these studies and articles are available even online for free. So nobody can claim that their ignorance is due to lack of information. Yet, it is one of the most repeated and rehashed false stories… and quoting the available (re)sources in order to enlighten the Masons still left in darkness has almost no effect. "But I heard if from an old Past Master…" is the usual rebuttal. Or rather excuse.

Some believe these myths and legends, some don't… and even authors that questioned the story, left sometimes open the possibility that it could turn out that the forget-me-not story was true. When it comes to contentious issues, we cannot go with such a lukewarm approach. There is enough historical evidence, written earlier by those who might have had first-hand experience of those times, completed with real research, that clearly prove the mythical character of certain elements of this folkloristic tale.

I happen to own such a lapel pin. And I got it many, many years ago from my mentor in Europe. And while I cherish his memory and the little token given to me, I now know that the beautiful and touching story that has been narrated so many times – simply doesn't withstand the examination of historians. It is understandable, to a certain extent, that idealistic Masonic brothers want to believe the inspiring narrative about the little blue flower. Even its name is evocative: forget not that you are a Mason!

It is not the intention here to re-tell the real story. It could be more useful for our weekly contemplations to think about why this story could stick with such a force. Because even a superficial look at how those authoritarian, dictatorial regimes functioned would reveal the simple fact that it was impossible to wear any kind of "pin" not sanctioned by the state and police, not to mention wearing a pin alluding to an outlawed organization. The ubiquitous police informant network and the very tight social control made everyone cautious and scared, nobody would dare to commit such a foolish, almost suicidal gesture.

It would be in the best interest of the Craft if we stopped spreading myths and legends about our own history. The verifiable facts in the history of Freemasonry are, most of the time, more fascinating than the fantasies that we so eagerly promote.

11 WHAT IS FREEMASONRY AND WHAT I AM DOING IN IT?

Let's put aside for a moment the lines we were told to learn as a simple answer to the question during our progression (a beautiful system of morality, veiled in allegory and illustrated by symbols).

Beyond that, how do we define for ourselves the essence of the Craft and our place in it?

Ever since speculative Freemasonry came to exist – and that's a topic worth pondering on its own – there have been plenty of the definitions and descriptions. We could just pick one of those fancy sentences and go with it, as we often do when outsiders, the non-Masons, ask about it. More often than not we try to give them a few words that are easy to understand and digest.

But today and this week we are not dealing with those outsiders, we try instead to look deep inside our soul, inside our most intimate convictions and thoughts: what is the Freemasonry that I am part of? What does it mean for me? Most likely everyone's path to become a Mason was different: from curiosity to family traditions, our initial reasons could be as various as the idea of what it would provide for us, namely from intellectual challenge to spiritual fulfillment and beyond.

There are no good answers and bad answers. YOUR answer is unique to you because your thoughts and your own life philosophy are unique – no two human beings are identical, and even identical twins think differently. That's why it is important for each Mason to be able to define our gentle Craft from his own perspective, with his own words.

A small clarification: it is often quoted (while nobody knows where it originated) that Freemasonry is different for everyone, implying a wide open – postmodernist – interpretation which would lead us to a subjectivism that is not desirable. If it were so open to personal and subjective interpretation or understanding, then how could it unite millions of members around the globe under the banners of the same ideal? Doesn't that fact point to something (and this undefined term is deliberate here!) that must be there for all of us to be bound in this fraternal tie?

The other slogan that needs to be rejected right here is the "sausage-making theory" – *you get out what you put in*. I call it this way because I know from my ancestors how the sausage is made: you put into that machine ground meat and out comes the same ground meat. Nothing really changed, except for the shape: the same ground meat is pressed into an intestine called casing…

But let's get back to this week's soul-searching: what is Freemasonry and what I am doing in it?

12 HISTORY AND BEGINNINGS

With so many ideas and (conspiracy) theories surrounding our Craft, it is not surprising to see so many confused Masons spreading false information about Freemasonry. Mostly unaware of this, they also contribute greatly to the misinformation of those who buy into such ideas. Freshly initiated Masons and Past Masters seem to be equally ignorant when it comes to history, facts, affiliation of famous people and other "popular" topics.

Just because two things look similar, it doesn't mean they are organically related. Consider this trivial example.

While bricks from clay have been made already in ancient Mesopotamia, probably in Babylon... today's brick factories are not direct descendants of those artisans thousands of years ago. Yes, the basic idea is the same: dig up, mould and shape the clay into a parallelepipedon(!), let it dry and then burn or bake it in fire. We (I mean the modern archaeologists) have found traces of such bricks during archaeological discoveries. In the village of my grandparents in Transylvania, the Gypsies (known today as Rroma) were the traditional clay brick manufacturers. They even have a clan named after this trade! Does this make them the "descendants" of the Babylonian brick-makers?

Did they inherit some kind of magic and secret knowledge from the ancient brick-manufacturers and through the Rroma was this secret insight being passed down to the Clay Brick Association of Canada? Anybody claiming such a connection would be laughed at and considered nuts.

Why can then the claim that today's modern Freemasonry originated in Noah's time or who knows when in the immemorial times of unwritten history… be seriously discussed by some Masons? Are we really thinking that the forced labour working on the Tower of Babel or the Temple of King Solomon were in any way the forerunners of modern English Masonry of the 18th century?

13 PRINCE HALL - SCHISM NO. 2

Once I heard a story about a former Lieutenant Governor of Ontario, a certain Hon. Lincoln Alexander, the first Black member in our parliament, the first black Lieutenant Governor who was a Mason. One of the past grand masters of Ontario was his friend, but they couldn't sit together in a lodge, because the Grand Master was from the "white" Masonry, while Lincoln Alexander from a Prince Hall lodge. And none of them could do anything about it.

Before moving to this continent, I have to admit, I didn't know about Prince Hall Masonry. Maybe I had heard something, but I can't recall paying too much attention. Generations grew up in the fifties and sixties of the past century in Eastern Europe without ever seeing a non-white man in real life. Of course, we had seen them in the movies, we knew about their existence (we all loved the then famous and acclaimed novel *Uncle Tom's Cabin* by Harriet Beecher Stowe) but we didn't have a first-hand experience.

The Eastern Bloc in Europe (a conveniently vague name for the former communist countries under the Soviet influence) ideologically fought for the equality of people, equality of races, equality of sexes, etc. As we all know from Orwell, some were more equal than others... nevertheless even bad ideologies can imprint great ideas on the mind of the young and innocent, so with the mandatory Bolshevik brainwashing, we also got this idea of racial equality, equality of sexes and so on. We somehow thought that the civil rights movement in that faraway country of "America" was the right thing to do. Interestingly, despite what some school boards think nowadays on this continent, literary works like *Huckleberry Finn* or *To Kill a Mockingbird*, made us very, very accepting of the idea of equal rights for Black people: we loved those non-white characters from the books that used the *now* dreaded N-word.

That idea of equality never went away, so as a young Mason discovering the rampant racial discrimination in the fraternity that I so idealistically loved and cherished – was a sad moment. It made me feel very uncomfortable and perturbed. By that time, I've met men and women of colour and as a novice Mason I really thought we were a universal brotherhood of educated like-minded men.[6] I already knew of the French "irregulars". That they were not real Masons, even though they thought they were. I grew up disliking them (the French) for historical reasons, but that wasn't as shocking as realizing that Black men were forced to create their own, racially segregated, Masonic system.

At the time of this writing there are forty-one Prince Hall Grand Lodges.

Let's use this week to research how many of those forty-one are recognized by our own "mainstream" (a.k.a. white) Grand Lodge?

---

[6] In Europe the lodges have fewer uneducated men; it is a long-standing tradition to try to attract the intellectual elite of the country.

14 ON ORIGINS

For centuries it has been accepted that in the medieval cathedral-building guilds, which used to store their tools in "lodges" adjacent to the big projects (some of them lasted couple of hundred years), certain curious gentlemen asked to be admitted... and one day these non-operative "masons" became the majority in the house and took over the lodges – and there we have today's Freemasonry. It is called the *transition theory*. Actually, Scotland's history has some evidence to consider this idea. Not really elsewhere...

Then there was this, somewhat similar theory positing that fugitive knights (and we are talking about the most famous-infamous order, the Templars) mingled with stonemasons, some even think they, the knights, taught them the secrets of the Gothic vaulted architecture, and the guilds and (again) lodges of the masons became a perfect hiding place for the persecuted wealthy and perhaps a bit heretical knights, who brought esoteric (oriental?) knowledge into these assemblies, together with some mandatory secrecy, and today's Freemasons are all descendants of this secret lineage.

Disregarding the more fantasist ideas of tracing the

Craft's origins back to biblical times (prebiblical Noah times?) and unsubstantiated Egyptian legends combined with obscure "Eastern" mystery-schools, we are left with little factual history, however our literature is rich in fascinating ideas about our origins. I enjoy reading those as much as anybody else, although my skeptical brain often tries to spoil the joy...

In this century more uncomfortable theories appeared. I call them "uncomfortable" because they go against any glorious ancestry and legendary origins, and bring everything down to the ground level of realpolitik. Like the theory that speculated that the newly installed Hanoverian dynasty (from the early 1700s) and their Whig-party supporters, together with the French Huguenot immigrants established in England, desirous of religious tolerance and freedom from persecution, created a brand **new organization** to serve their mundane interests – meanwhile borrowing the symbolism (tools and basic moral teachings) of the operative craftsmen[7]. And this new institution started to spread like wildfire across the globe, although mainly in the territories ruled by the ever-expanding British Empire. There is quite compelling evidence to support this idea, and more and more books and studies elaborate on the theory, discussing it from different angles. It should be discussed separately that the Freemasonry which crossed the Channel to Europe soon became a completely different intellectual movement.

Besides the well-known cliché found at the introduction of the usual Masonic "histories" – *no one really knows where Freemasonry originated from* – the real question by now really is: do we want to learn our own history or we prefer all kind of fairy tales? Which theory is preferred in your circles?

---

[7] Berman, Ric. *Foundations of Modern Freemasonry: The Grand Architects — Political Change and the Scientific Enlightenment*, 1714 - 1740. 2011

15 ORGANIZATIONS OF MASONS IN THE PAST?

Roman Collegia
Builders had organized themselves from the ancient times – so goes the other "argument" wanting to give the pedigree of antiquity to our Craft. Therefore, and here comes the logical leap: we are descendants of all those organizations, like the Roman Collegia. But are we? There is no evidence, only speculation that elements of the collegia in the Roman Empire might have survived and constituted the base of the medieval guilds in Europe.

We know there was a *Collegium Fabrorum* (of builders) but also *Collegium Lupanariorum*… In case you missed the Latin class: it means brothel-keepers' guild. Just a reminder that we should be careful whom we associate with.

The Germanic Steinmetzen and the French Compagnonnage
Those were early systems of transmitting the knowledge and trade "secrets" of the German stone-cutters (*Stein* = stone), and of different trade skills in France. While the former is extinct, the latter is still in existence in France,

providing a hands-on education and initiation for apprentices. These systems, however, never outgrew their homeland and did not become a worldwide system of fraternal organizations. They are extremely interesting to study and to understand – but it would be difficult to accept them as the medieval precursors of modern Freemasonry.

All kind of guilds around the world and modern unions and "brotherhoods"

From the guilds of the Middle Ages, like that of the tailors or shoemakers, regulating that specific trade in the jurisdiction of a town or city, up to the modern unions (sometimes misleadingly called brotherhoods), all were professional organizations meant to protect their own self-interests. The guilds, as self-regulatory bodies, were establishing the path from apprentice to journeyman to 'master', a rank achieved by making and presenting to those in charge their 'masterpiece', the proof of their skills. These requirements were similar, regardless of the trade. After long years of apprenticeship, the young man went on a journey (hence: journeyman) sometimes just to other towns, sometimes even to foreign countries. After returning they could apply to become a master member, a kind of self-employed tradesman of the time. The guilds, just like unions and professional organizations today, tried to maintain their monopoly on production and their authority to decide who can practice in their territory.

Again, similarities don't mean kinship. By definition, any initiatic order – from ancient times till today – will show similarities: the structures and methods of such organizations are related. They have a ritual, they follow a ceremonial procedure during which they bring the novice "outsider" inside the circle of members that were previously initiated. Of course, there will be steps and ways of doing things that would strike us as 'similar'. But those similarities come from the nature of these things.

16 MYSTICISM AND HISTORY

The second half of the 19th century and the beginning of the next one was the era of abundant interpretations of the Masonic symbols. Obviously, it was in part in tune with the *Zeitgeist* of the era: anything and everything deemed *occult, mystic, esoteric, spiritual, metaphysical* – in other words beyond the rational intellect – became of interest. What was to be termed as *Western esotericism* has been in full swing of its development.

Esotericism was regarded or interpreted as encompassing a universal, secret tradition or the hidden knowledge, and also, as a different worldview situated on the opposing end of our generally accepted "rational" worldview. While studying Western esotericism, or any kind esotericism in general, has become by now an accepted and legitimate academic field of research, the era under our microscope wasn't known as the epitome of rigorous scientific research in this field. It is known to be one of the most prolific periods producing the most "esoteric" schools around every corner. Most of them, resembling the earlier "historic schools", used to claim all kinds of legendary and mythical ancestry and precursors, creating an abundance of made-up legends and secret knowledge schools. In this plethora of quasi-ancient esoteric schools and organizations, and theories, it was and still is quite difficult to separate the wheat from the chaff.

In this regard, interpretations, and re-interpretations of Freemasonry and of *Masonic symbolism* in peculiar, were aligned with the trends in vogue, and those ideas became influential on our self-image as Masons. And because this territory of the human knowledge was (maybe still is) outside of the positivist scientific approach and its Baconian roots of evidence-based *natural philosophy*, the realm was wide open to any graphomaniac blessed with rich fantasy and some superficial knowledge of the ancient or medieval esoteric heritage. Where there weren't any, imaginary "ancestors" were easily invented since the field was beyond the limits of the academic exigencies.

A closer look would reveal astonishing similarities with how *Masonic history* has been treated for a long time, when well-intended non-historian Masons wrote (hi)stories for Masons, meanwhile the academia neglected the social implications of Freemasonry. Allegedly, writing about Freemasonry as an established historian meant endangering one's credibility as a scholar. So, in this 'vacuum', the self-appointed Masonic historians created a fantasy-land, which turned out to be a very fertile soil for our own urban legends.

Even in our present days, only a few distinguished Masonic scholars moved away from this trend and abandoned *hagiographic*[8] history to be replaced by solid academic research and source analysis. The average Mason is still behind, and the collective self-image perpetuates the earlier fabulations and mythical theories, presenting an eclectic mix of philosophical roots evidenced by our texts (charges, rituals, lectures), the imaginary predecessors of times immemorial, and the urban legends of modern popular culture.

---

[8] Péter, Róbert, editor. *British Freemasonry, 1717-1813*. Routledge, 2016. *Bowker*. vol. 1. p.xiv

Starting from the 1940s, in the beginning sporadically, and later with more frequency, scholarly works discussing the Craft's origins, its religious-philosophical roots, its real history embedded in the larger social and historical context became the norm – at least in academic circles. However, these new works and discoveries didn't "trickle down" to the lodges level. With the exception of dedicated research lodges and societies, or the intellectually focused "observant" lodges, these results and the scientific approach towards our own history and philosophy are rare, almost non-existent in everyday Masonry.

The unfortunate situation is sustained in part by the way "Masonic education" is practiced in many lodges across the continent. Quite often it comes as an afterthought, required by the higher echelons of Freemasonry, and the lodge diligently conforms to it by assigning always the same poor brother to present a "short" paper about a Masonic topic. Rarely are those the results of independent research or original thought, because it became admissible to rehash old articles, old ideas, and subjects, originating from that dubious era of Masonic "science" and "esotericism"… contributing to the eternal re-enforcement and perpetuation of the rancid topics of our lore. Masonic literature from the second half of the 20th century, not to mention the present, 21st century doesn't exist in these regurgitated lectures.

When will the Craft discover the new trends in Masonic research, the really important new developments in the academic publications? It seems that we are always a hundred years behind. Why did the "interpretation" of Masonic symbols and hidden meaning stop in the last almost 100 years?[9]

---

[9] Some of the most relevant Masonic authors from that era:Albert Mackey 1807-1881; Albert Pike 1809-1891; Robert Freke Gould 1836 – 1915; Walter Leslie Wilmshurst 1867 – 1939; Carl Harry Claudy 1879 – 1957

17 ON TIME

Time is not of specific concern in Masonic lore and literature. Except the overused phrase "from time immemorial" little or no attention is paid to the concept of time in itself.

From ancient mythologies till the latest time-space continuum theories, the concept of time has been in the centre of our beliefs and philosophies. Today we are more focused on the "measurable" time, for which the ancient Greeks (who else) used the word Kronos – which can be easily recognized in chronology, chronometer, chronicles etc. As Masons we are concerned with the exact time of our gatherings (*the lodge will be tyled exactly at 7:30 pm*), the length of our meetings, and the time requirements of our duties. All related to our omnipresent calendars, from the earlier weekly planners to the different phone apps.

We rarely think that the same old Greeks had another word and a different concept, too. As some say, this was about "deep time", something that was concerned about the person's immersion in a moment, when seemingly the profound experience of a moment (be it a perfect sunset, a magnificent landscape, or a bond with a fellow human) makes one to feel as if time is not ticking (we all know that time is not ticking, only our man-made gizmos to measure Kronos). This "deep time" was known for the ancient Greeks as *Kairos*…

Back to the lodge. What kind of time do we experience in our lodges? Is it slower or faster than the "flight" of time outside of the lodge? (As a side note: There is this idea that as we age time in our perception becomes "faster", i.e. a year seems shorter and faster when we are sixty compared to how we live through a year when we are six years old.)

Presumably, if we have an outstanding experience in a lodge, time should go "deep" and stand still (Kairos) – to allow us to fully immerse into that extraordinary moment which cannot be repeated unlike the start time (Kronos) of the regular meeting which is occurring and re-occurring on our chronometers.

There is also this opposite idea that says: in a good lodge, during a good meeting time goes so fast that we don't even notice it. On a personal perception level this might be just as valid as the earlier concept of slowing down.

Ponder your time in lodge without adding any modifier (good, bad, boring, happy etc.) – think only about the time. As a physical and philosophical thing. Is time "happening" outside or inside us?

18 GRAND ORIENT OF FRANCE – SCHISM NO. 3

One day in the year 1877 the biggest and oldest "Grand Lodge" in France, known by the name of Grand Orient of France (GOF – meaning the Great East), at the insistence of a Protestant minister(!), decided to remove the requirement for the belief in a Supreme Being for its candidates, and no longer displayed the Bible on the altar/pedestal in the lodge. To be historically more precise: it was left to the private lodges to decide whether they use the Bible or not. As for the individual Masons, GOF considered that the *liberty of conscience* must prevail, consequently, the faith of their members (or the lack of it) is a private, personal matter, and no institution should dictate it or interfere with it.

This is the usual short version of the story given in most of our general Masonic histories.

Before anyone screams "sacrilege" seeing the phrase *liberty of conscience* thinking it to be an euphemism for atheist, it is good to look back at the basic document that laid the foundation of our modern Freemasonry as we know it: the 1723 Constitution says that while in earlier times Masons were expected to follow their "state religion", it was now (in 1723) considered more expedient only to oblige them to that religion in which all men agree, that is, to be good men and true, men of honour and honesty[10]. Some say the lack of mention of the mandatory belief in a Supreme Being is deliberate; others consider it just an example of missing the obvious: often what is perceived as given and generally accepted, is not mentioned because it is part of the worldview.

On the other hand, it is almost ironic that thirty years before the "atheist" move, in 1849, the Grand Orient ordered all its lodges to display the Bible on the altar. That grand body did other strange things, too. In 1869 it declared that Black men (or any non-white for that matter) can be admitted in Masonic lodges, and recognized a group of such Masons in Louisiana – in consequence, that state and a few more American jurisdictions withdrew their recognition of the GOF... And then came the removal of the requirement to believe in a Supreme Being.

In the aftermath, the "universal" brotherhood experienced its third biggest schism, which exists even in our days. The Grand Lodges and obediences that align themselves with the Grand Orient of France (GOF) are considered by the self-titled regular obediences "irregular",

---

[10] "A Mason is oblig'd by his Tenure, to obey the moral Law; and if he rightly understands the Art, he will never be a stupid Atheist nor an irreligious Libertine. But though in ancient Times Masons were charg'd in every Country to be of the Religion of that Country or Nation, whatever it was, yet 'tis now thought more expedient only to oblige them to that Religion in which all Men agree, leaving their particular Opinions to themselves; that is, to be good Men and true, or Men of Honour and Honesty, by whatever Denominations or Persuasions they may be distinguish'd; whereby Masonry becomes the Center of Union, and the Means of conciliating true Friendship among Persons that must have remain'd at a perpetual Distance." – quote from James Anderson's *Constitution of 1723*.

"Continental", "Liberal" or "Latin"… although they like to self style themselves as "adogmatic". Which (almost) implies that on the other side of the spectrum are the "dogmatic" obediences. And that would make all the regular Grand Lodges *dogmatic*. (Language is a funny thing, can carry lots of judgement…)

In consequence, we have two main streams or types of male Freemasonry around the world: the "regular" one that is recruiting its members from among the theists (believers in a deity), and the "irregular" (self-styled "adogmatic") one, which accepts atheists and believers alike.

An important distinction here should be the often missed detail that atheism is not a GOF "requirement". Theoretically, every regular Mason, having a belief in a Supreme Being, would not be excluded or stopped from joining a GOF lodge just based on this criterion.

This schism is another proof, if needed, that there is no "universal" world-wide organization of Freemasons – only many different Freemasonries. In plural! One would permit any man to join, provided they were a man of good character, the other recruits its members from among the same men of good character, but asking to be believers in a deity.

Why is it that *the most tolerant fraternity* in the world cannot even get these two factions to talk to each other and respect each other?

19 WHY INITIATION?

Every initiatory ceremony or ritual has one single purpose: to share with the newly admitted member (the initiated) knowledge about the sacred. Those who do not belong to the inner circle are not initiated, they are profane – not knowing the sacred. From the shamanistic Central-Asian cultures to the Native Aboriginals of the Americas as well as the various religious orders… all have a well-designed ceremony (a scenario, if you will) to solemnly bring the profane candidate from the state of darkness (ignorance, lack of knowledge) to the elevated state of being initiated, where he or she receives the light of the secret – and sacred – knowledge.

Freemasons will recognize in the sentences above allusions to their rituals. However, there is almost no initiatic order that wouldn't feel the same way: that the references above describe their own initiation rituals. And that's exactly the point: all organizations that have such a character, will present similar traits because there is no other way to do an initiation. To share the insiders' sacred knowledge one has to go through events and stages that will prepare and enable the person to receive the same insider information.

Let's think of a few elements that are commonly found in initiatory ceremonies: special clothing (or lack of), solitude before the ceremony to contemplate, a guide that conducts the candidate through the events, and a group of insiders participating in a role play like a ritual and sharing certain sacred esoteric knowledge with the newly admitted member.

Note. Initiation should never be mistaken for the so-called "hazing" so popular in college fraternities and sororities.

20 EVERYBODY WAS A MASON…

…or so we like to think. From the ancient Egyptian pharaohs to astronauts and kings, to presidents and famous artists – anyone can be suspected of being a Freemason in the eyes of the conspiracy believers. And of ignorant Masons as well.

Let's explain this logical fallacy (or failure) in a crystal clear manner: if there was no *modern* Freemasonry prior to the lodges that existed in the British Isles, then there were no Freemasons before that. Therefore, no Biblical characters could be claimed as Masons. Also, Leonardo da Vinci wasn't a Mason – no matter what we read in a fictional book. (Definition of fiction - literature in the form of prose[…] that describes *imaginary events and people*.) Emphasis mine to warn the reader! Neither was Pepin the Short, or Charlemagne. The same for the Knights Templar.

The more you read about the history of our Craft, the more you will develop that "sixth sense" for discerning the difference between factual events and fantasy stories.

As for living celebrities – the very first rule that I learned as a Mason was this: I can state publicly about myself that I am a Freemason, but I can never ever say anything like that about a brother of mine. So, stop guessing and naming living personalities as Freemasons! Wait until they die.

21 DISCRIMINATION AND JUDGMENT

We claim that we don't discriminate. We are an organization, fraternity or whatever you call it, which does not discriminate. Too bad it is not true. First of all, we discriminate against half of the population of the globe: females are not allowed in our lodges. Next, we discriminate based on faith or belief: if men willing to join our ranks do not believe in some kind of Supreme Being, a Supreme Creator of the universe, they are out. In some jurisdictions, this faith-based discrimination is even more severe because they only allow people who believe in a *monotheistic* deity — or Supreme Being. Polytheism or deism is considered questionable in a number of jurisdictions. And we also discriminate in quite a subjective way, because we do not want men who are not good. As the cliché goes we take **good men and make them better**. We tend to forget the first part of this mantra — *taking good men*, not any men, not just some men, they must be good, even before we consider to prepare them for initiation. As we see, there's a lot of discrimination going on in our organization.

Next, we say *"oh, we don't judge, we are non judgmental…"* This is the biggest nonsense (to avoid using harsher words) that crept in from the general politically correct mindset into our Craft. Consider this: when a seeker[11] applies to become a member (ideally, when the lodge is ready to hand him an application form), he submits the application, signed by his sponsor(s). The following step is that the Worshipful Master sends out a an investigation committee to meet the applicant. Their duty, actually is *to judge the character* of the individual that applied for membership and report back to the Worshipful Master and to the lodge. Practically, they are the eyes and the ears of the master of the lodge! Their mission is to judge, to judge — what else? — the character of the applicant. "Guarding the West Gate" means judging the character of the man knocking on the door of the lodge.

In some other jurisdictions, outside of North America, the members of the investigative committee usually don't go together to visit an applicant, but each member of the committee sets up his own appointment to visit the applicant at his home, to meet his family as well if he has one, and they have long and in-depth conversation about a lot of topics, way beyond the mandatory list of questions that the lodge or grand lodge would provide. The goal is to know their way of thinking, their worldview, their mentality, as much as possible about the man, not only a jovial chit-chat about the weather and the latest football game. Of course, they will notice that the applicant likes to watch sports, but that's a very minor detail when it comes to decide whether he fits or not into the lodge (unless it is a sport-focused affinity lodge).

These are only two of the *perpetuating myths* in our lodges, i. e. that we don't discriminate and that we don't judge. Well, the moment we stopped to discriminate and to judge, everything we think essential regarding freemasonry would be gone. Do we really want that?

---

[11] seeker - in some jurisdictions the men interested in joining the Craft are called "seeker of the light".

22 FOUNDING FATHERS AND BREWERS

It is a well-known fact that the ideals taught in Masonic lodges have been implemented as the basic tenets of a few new countries created by Masons and like-minded individuals who left the old world to build a better one. The most important ideals for them were: equality and religious freedom for all men, a *utopian* world of harmony, peace and freedom. (Hat tip to Sir Francis Bacon who wasn't a Freemason.)

In other places the principles already practiced in the lodges (e.g. the Rule of Law, parliamentarism - to use modern terminology - where everyone has an equal vote, democracy and equal rights) became the ideals to be imitated in the whole society.

In short, many political institutions of the modern era were influenced by Freemasons and their ideals and practices. This doesn't mean that every adherent of those ideas was a Mason. Thomas Paine, the influential "celebrity" of the era, even wrote a history of Masonry, but he was not a documented member of the Craft. Out of the 56 men that signed the (American) Declaration of

Independence only nine were Masons: nine out of the fifty six, one in six, 16 percent!

In Canada, we also had a number of Masons at the birth of the Confederation in 1867. More interestingly, all three of the famous Canadian beer brewers were also Freemasons: John *Labatt*, Alexander *Keith*, John *Molson*. Should we say that these are (or were) Masonic beers?

23 CAN WOMEN BE FREEMASONS?

It depends on whom you ask. There are jurisdictions where the ritual explicitly forbids their members to participate in the process of making a woman a Mason. N.B[12].: Logic 101 would explain that that sentence implies that women are and were initiated into the Craft, but the male Masons are not allowed to be part of the ceremony. Many of those who took this obligation, later might develop a belief that even mentioning the existence of female Freemasonry is a sacrilege. Obligations in other parts of the world are not written in the same way.

At the other end of the spectrum are the (at least two) obediences of "regular" Masonry for Women. They both have their headquarters in England, so it should not be surprising that the Grand Lodge of England, the UGLE, has a civilized relationship with them – although not recognizing those bodies *masonically*. Hence the quotation mark around regular.

A quick detour from the main question to clarify the types of relations which exist between Grand Lodges and similar bodies. Two such (grand) bodies can *recognize* each

---

[12] Latin: *nota bene* – pay special attention

other, and be *in amity*. Mutual amity. Normally, that means they regard each other as "regular", and mutual visitation is allowed. If a Grand Lodge (Grand Orient) is considered "irregular" – then there is no recognition, and visitation is forbidden.

The UGLE acknowledging women's Freemasonry, they *acknowledge* the existence, they even admit that the women's ritualistic work might be "regular"... except for the grave irregularity of being women. Despite this irregularity, they often share lodge buildings, and also participate together in non-ritualistic social events and public displays.

The *university scheme*, an initiative to popularize Freemasonry among students, is such an event, where male and female Masons both try to attract new members from the universities. This kind of more tolerant attitude and sharing (renting?) facilities has started to become more widespread than some misogynistic men like to admit.

Back to the initial dilemma: in some places there are grand lodges that allow both male and female lodges, though not mixed lodges. The first such organization that claimed to be Freemasonry and initiated both men and women in their lodges, was *Le Droit Humain* – an international obedience of the so-called co-Masonry. (In many languages they are simply called mixed Freemasonry.)

In the historical narrative of the Anglo-American Masonry there are anecdotal stories about a few ladies, in the past, who have been accepted into the ranks of Freemasons... by sheer accident. For example, when a lady witnessed the ceremony, the gentlemen, instead of killing her, made her a Mason, taking upon her the obligation to not divulge the "secrets."

What is less spoken about is the fact that in earlier centuries the Lodges of Adoption actually were a popular form of Masonry among women. More recent historical studies based on documents (and less on self-perpetuating legends), provide ample evidence for the existence of female Freemasonry[13].

It is understandable that mainly for historical reasons and due to the traditionalist nature of the Craft, Freemasonry is predominantly a male organization. It is also known that men start behaving differently if females are also present in a group: the dynamics change and the testosterone prevails…

In the 21st century, those that are more comfortable being in a men only lodge where male camaraderie defines the social aspects, should be allowed to continue as they wish. Women not only should be allowed to join their – women-only – lodges, but also be recognized, since they act by and adhere to the same moral principles as the male lodges do. (A reminder: they use the same rituals teaching the same moral lessons as we do!) As for the mixed lodges? Who are we to tell any man on this planet what kind of "Masonic" group he can join? Or any woman, for that matter.

What if your wife joined a Masonic lodge?

---

[13] see: Anon., *Womens Masonry or Masonry by Adoption* (London: Hookham, 1765);
Snoek, Jan. *Initiating Women in Freemasonry*. BRILL, 2012;
Önnerfors, Andreas. *Freemasonry: A Very Short Introduction*. 2017. Bowker.

24 ON ELITE(S)

The word elite "comes from *eligere* (to choose Latin): French : chosen... it used to mean the "the best" i.e. a choice or select body, the best part,"... nothing about money and wealth and ruling classes. (That came later.) In this regard, regarding the best, we used to think and talk about the 'intellectual' and 'spiritual' elite of a nation or society – the thinkers and leaders of a community that we looked up to and respected and admired... sometimes even honoured.

Until recently the word "elite" did NOT mean the richest one percent of the population - which is nowadays the predominant interpretation of the word among younger people. While I was taught back in Europe that Freemasons used to "recruit" their members from the cultural elite of the country, in my chosen land (pun intended) a young Mason can state with a degree of indignation that we are not the elite... almost being offended that someone assumed Freemasons were the spiritual-intellectual elite of the place. No way, we are not, he replied.

Interestingly, when we are in the mood for boasting about the Craft, we always bring up all the famous people from history who were members. (Sometimes even those whose membership in a lodge cannot be proven.) From the first president of the USA (George Washington) to the genius composer Wolfgang Amadeus Mozart, from Winston Churchill to Louis Armstrong, we all have a long list of "great people" who were Freemasons. Yet, don't we consider them to be the "elite" of their times?

Sad side note. Celebrities are among the contemporaries we often try to associate our fraternity with, mistakenly thinking them to be the elite.

Do you want elite people or celebrities in your lodge?

25 FREEMASONS IN THE BIBLE

Everybody knows, including non-Masons, that most of the symbols, characters, stories that we tell in our ceremonies (rituals) are based on Biblical texts. For some that's a proof of Freemasonry being a "Christian" organization, for others these rituals are just like any parables of the Old Testament: stories taken from a source and then shaped and morphed into a role-play to convey moral teachings and to instill inspiration for the betterment of our virtues. (Note: there are absolutely no references to the New Testament in the ritual!)

One of the central characters in our stories is King Solomon and his temple. It is very interesting that in the light of the latest research, the metaphor of the "temple", especially that of the Temple of Jerusalem, as the temple of wisdom [*templum sapientiae*], the temple of the encyclopedic knowledge [*templum encyclopediae*] was a returning topos – a traditional topic formula in the decades just before the formation of the first known Grand Lodge in 1717. The symbolism of the temple and in a larger context, the symbolism of "New Jerusalem" is present in English rhetoric since Sir Francis Bacon...

Freemasonry, or more exactly, the authors of the first

books and rules and of mythology just adapted the existing literary themes for their purposes. It is worth noting that 300 years ago the stories of the Bible, of classic Greek and Roman mythology and literature were the basis of what we would call education. So the easiest way to convey a message – be it of morals or other spiritual content – was by using the well-known stories, parables, metaphors, and symbolism.

However, there are no Freemasons in the Bible.

Meanwhile in the centre of our allegorical teachings stands the story of erecting King Solomon's Temple, embellished with certain fictional elements to fit our purpose, but those builders were not "Freemasons" in the modern sense of the word. The Hiramic legend is just that - a legend, a beautiful uplifting story of devotion, loyalty and dedication. Another day we shall contemplate on that addition to our rituals where Hiram became the central character.

Furthermore, all researchers agree that the hero in our Hiramic legend from the third degree of Craft Freemasonry, is not the same as the "bronze worker" mentioned in the Scripture. For some, this might come as a painful discovery: there is nothing about the life or - more importantly - the death of Hiram in the Bible.

26 DEVIATION

Religion and science, usually, come together in the same sentence only when the so-called creationists and evolutionists confront each other. From a regular Mason's perspective that debate is irrelevant, at least that's the generally accepted, though simplistic, argument. Let's assume that we really don't need to take sides in that discussion, mainly because membership in regular Masonry requires a belief in a "Supreme Being" – a deity of some kind, and that automatically implies the idea of creation of the world by a Great Architect of the Universe. (Again, a simplistic philosophical approach, but for now it can serve us well.) This requirement, to believe in a Supreme Being, happens at the first step, or even before making the first step in Masonry.

Next, when we already are inside, initiated into the Craft, at certain point in our Masonic journey we are encouraged to study the "hidden mysteries of nature and science". It is strongly related to the other instruction which tells us to persevere in the study of the seven liberal arts and sciences.

Here we have two very clear and direct teachings: one, that we must have a belief in the Great Architect of the

Universe, and on the other hand, we must diligently study "science" for our daily advancement in Freemasonry. Consequently, it is not too much of a stretch to think that religion and science occupy a central place in Masonic ideology and philosophy.

Personally, I consider dictionaries and encyclopedias published by reputable universities and publishers a reliable source of knowledge. Of course, they are just a starting point to find clues for which direction to go in with our research. Hence, proposing a discussion in a Masonic group about these topics – namely, religion and science – would seem worth consideration. Yes, everybody is aware that there is a long-standing prohibition on discussing religious topics in a lodge, but to analyze and dissect a draft of a scientific article from a future encyclopedia of philosophy… maybe should not be considered a "deviation" from Masonic topics.

Yet, such prohibition can happen. Do you think that the general anti-intellectualism experienced in society at large, has also started to appear in our Craft? Isn't this antithetical to our claim of encouraging learning and philosophical contemplation?

When was the last time you discussed religion and science with your brothers?

27 ON SECRECY

Is it normal that a generation grew up without knowing that their fathers were Masons?

It is a valid question since there are many stories about adult men discovering that other men in their families – fathers, grandfathers, uncles etc. – were members of the Craft, yet they had no knowledge of it until they, eventually, joined a lodge.

When I was initiated in one of the Eastern European Grand Lodges resurrected on the ruins of the communist regimes imposed by the Soviets, I was told that in addition to the modes of recognition there was only one other rule about secrecy: I could tell people that I was a Mason. But under no circumstances was I allowed to reveal the membership of any other brother, unless they expressly agreed. As strange as it might seem to an outsider, for those who experienced oppressive regimes and dictatorships outlawing Freemasonry, this was a very reasonable rule since it was my decision if I wanted to take the risk of "advertising" my belonging to the Craft, but I should not endanger my brother…

Unfortunately, this rule still has to be in effect in places where you can lose your job and livelihood if the authorities (or just bad people) find out that you are a Mason.

But why do we need unnecessary secrecy that conceals even from our family members the fact of being a member of the Craft in free and democratic places, where the membership in a Masonic lodge is not, or should not be seen as something to hide? Sometimes family members of such secretive Masons recall their father or grandfather saying, it was secret, 'I cannot tell you anything'. Some present-day authors, analyzing such stories, may say that the father or grandfather at the centre of that story was not properly mentored in the Masonic lore, and he had no idea what he could and what he couldn't tell his family. Consequently, instead of showing their insecurity and lack of knowledge, they decided that everything was "secret". A mystery to conceal and never to reveal.

At the end, these Masons caused more harm than good with their unreasonably secretive attitude, and this secrecy might be one of the reasons of the dwindling numbers in the lodges of North America. (Not that the small number of lodges or Freemasons is a bad thing per se, we just mention it here because it seems to be everybody's concern. But maybe this is a thought for another week.)

In most jurisdictions today the only secrets are the modes of recognition, signs, and passwords. We can – should? – talk about most of the rest with our friends and family. Aren't you proud of what you do in the lodge and in the Craft? Aren't you proud of what you learned and experienced that made you a better man? Isn't your participation in the Masonic ceremony and ritual a fulfilling life experience worth sharing with the ones you love?

If the answer is yes, how much secrecy do we really need?

28 THE SHAME

I am a Mason raised in Europe in a different language with a different ritual. I have lived in three provinces of Canada and was active masonically in two. And I was elected to sit in the East so everything seems to be fine.

Well, not quite.

Yes, I achieved a very important milestone in every Mason's journey, to be elected and installed as the Master of the lodge, to employ and instruct our brethren in Masonry. And, honestly, that seemed unimaginable when I first stepped into a lodge in this great country. Yet, it happened. This would be the bright side.

On the dark side, I have witnessed religious intolerance and Christian bigotry, I've heard racist jokes about 'coloured' (what a crazy word!) Masons – behind their backs, of course –, and heard otherwise good brothers mocking the foreign accent of foreign-born Masons. Yeah, mine, too, but that's not the point.

That I didn't slap anybody making fun of my accent could be perceived as something positive. In this one instance I was able to subdue my passions. Or maybe I was just too cowardly to stand up and confront them…

We often do this in the name of misunderstood "brotherly love" when we let the bad apples get away with character flaws.

But for not standing up and not kicking out the racist and bigoted members - I am ashamed even at this very moment while writing this.

29 ON RITUAL

The world famous Little Prince of Saint-Exupery one day met the fox, who told him:

'We all need rituals.'
'What is a ritual?' said the little prince.
'Something else that is frequently neglected,' said the fox.
It's what makes one day different from the other days, one hour different from the other hours...'

A very simple concept: we need to make one hour different from the other hours. Or maybe make a whole day different – namely the day of the regular meeting of the lodge. Sometimes there are voices that question the necessity of ritual(s). In Masonry and in general. Most likely, they don't understand the function of the ritual - or any ritualistic event. Somewhat along the lines of the friendly little fox we can say that the role of the ritual is to delimit the outer profane world from our inner workings, and to create that *sacred space* — a different realm — where like-minded men come together to contemplate and work.

The reason we find so many similarities in the different rituals across cultures and languages is that they always aim for the same spiritual purpose: to create a shared experience for the "insiders", i.e. the members of that community — which in our case is the lodge — behind closed doors, while the outer guard is securing that meeting. The secrecy (closed door) is not for hiding anything, it is for the exclusion of the non-initiated outer world. Let's replace the inner and outer word-pair with a Latin one: esoteric vs. exoteric. The ritual is how we convey *esoteric* knowledge and symbolism. Even if we would allow any outsider to come in and participate (watch it), everything, every element of the ritual would be meaningless for that person.

It is the ritual of Freemasonry that sets us apart from any other fraternity or organization.

In some jurisdictions the participants have to memorize everything, and they have to "deliver" it, using the techniques of rhetoric presenting an elaborate role play; in other places, the text of the ritual is partially read. One can find heated debates on both sides. We should all follow the traditions of our jurisdiction – or, if brave enough, create our own new traditions.

The only measurement for the efficiency of the ritual should be to measure the "sacredness" of the virtual space created by it. Since that cannot be "quantified" one must know when it is achieved.

You will know it when you know it.

30 FREETHINKERS OR CONFORMISTS

The word "freethinker" creates bad vibes in the perception of many people where certain conservative Christian traditions are predominant in society. Perhaps other cultures regard this intellectual stance with the same suspicion since freethought questions every accepted dogma and tradition.

There is, however, a group of men and women who like to think for themselves, to examine ruling belief systems and religious traditions by the light of reason and logic – and just as the name says: they think "free" from any preconceived idea. There was a time when I truly believed that each and every member of the so-called *intelligentsia*[14] was supposed to think for themselves. Or, at least to think…

On the other hand, the conservative religious point of view is that "freethinkers" equals atheists, consequently they are evil. We all know from history that for religious zealots, every person daring to deviate even an iota from the official dogma was regarded as a heretic.

---

[14] Originally from Latin roots, but in this form a word borrowed from Russian (*интеллигенция*).

Is today a freethinker considered a "heretic" by the ideals – or tenets – of Freemasonry?

The answer will depend on which myth of origin you prefer. Our beliefs in those myths rarely have anything to do with the facts. They are mostly adjusted to our own worldview to reflect not only our self-image but the place we think we occupy in this world. In other words, the real, or imaginary, role we assign to ourselves, or to the group we belong to, will define which intellectual tradition we ascribe to the Craft.

On one hand, there is the well-known charge where we admonish our newly admitted members to be law abiding decent citizens (subjects) of the governing status quo. There is nothing wrong with that... although not exactly a "revolutionary" attitude. On the other hand, there are the ideals "inculcated" in other Masonic streams, calling to fight against tyranny, to stand up for equality and the rights of the oppressed – clearly values aligned with the non-conformist freethinkers.

Paradoxically, in the same jurisdiction, more exactly in different Masonic bodies actually meeting in the same building, one can find both of these traditions: calling on the Mason for exemplary discharge of civil duties (i.e. never to subvert the peace and good order of society) and the next day calling on him to stand up against tyranny, to fight for the oppressed, for justice, for equity... The attentive reader will discover even the echoes of the slogans of the French revolution: *liberté, égalité, fraternité.*

Any Mason whose lodge is using a ritual originating from the old European continent (as opposed to those coming from the British Isles) or went through the "higher" degrees of the appendant bodies, could easily identify words and notions from the previous paragraph. Unfortunately, we never analyze the striking contradiction between the two "teachings". Somehow, our minds treat them in a comfortably compartmentalized way: one goes this way, the other that way, and the two are not related –

so we don't need to deal with them.

Let's put aside the free part for now and keep only the thinker. We must think, it is our moral and intellectual obligation to ponder controversial ideas, and then decide our position on that broad spectrum between conformism and free-thought.

31 ON MUSIC

Music is mentioned in our lectures being one of the seven liberal arts and sciences. We all are aware of the importance of music in our lives... and we might only differ over our taste and choice of genre. What we don't, or rarely, mention is that music is an integral part of many rituals in the human existence.

Consider the two beautiful examples presented below. They are very distant in time and space, yet they tell us something extremely important about the role of music.

"The Australian Aborigines, hunter-gatherers, while moving with the seasons to find animals to hunt, and plant materials to gather, call these paths song lines, and as they travel along their ancestral routes they sing the story of the journey and the sacred places along the way. Far from them, in Eastern Europe, among Ashkenazi Jews there are songs called nigun – a song of the Kabbalistic/Chassidic tradition, generally without words. Considered a path to higher consciousness and transformation of being.

"If words are the pen of the heart," taught a rabbi "then song is the pen of the soul."

The soul's pen, however, writes in the opposite direction from the heart's. While words carry meaning downwards from God's own primal consciousness into the minds of sages [...] to inscribe them upon human hearts, song carries the soul upwards to be absorbed within the Infinite Light. That is why nigun generally have no words." [15]

If only the music in our lodges had some resemblance to these magnificent examples of music in rituals!

Some jurisdictions and some lodges may fare better, and complement the Masonic ritualistic experience with songs or music. After all, beginning with Mozart, we have quite an honourable line of Masonic musicians and composers whose music could enliven the lodge ceremony.

At the opposite end of the musical spectrum is using modified lyrics of the Anglo-American Protestant *church hymnals*. It may seem a delicate and complicated issue to even talk about, but nobody can pretend the problem is nonexistent. First, and we hear this from people grown up and socialized in this culture, they say, if one wants to enjoy church hymnals, one can go to any Protestant denomination to worship with those songs. Secondly, a growing number of North American Masons are coming from a different background. For them, the "Anglo" Protestantism with its classical hymnals and odes is not familiar, and they tend to reject it.

It is easy to understand how we ended up with these songs. There was a time, just a couple of generations ago, when the majority of Masons came from traditional white Anglo-Saxon Protestant families, for whom the weekly church attendance was the norm. They all grew up singing those songs, and therefore, no huge effort was required from eager brothers of the Craft to adapt new (Masonic) lyrics to the already known melodies. They just needed to print the "new" text for the lodges, and in many lodges they still place such lyrics cards on the seats for members

---

[15] Tzvi Freeman, Music and Transformation. *Exodus Magazine*, issue 242, (January 2023). p.6.

and guests. But since the newer generations don't attend church regularly, their singing skills and knowledge of the hymnals are nil. This results in pathetic disturbing sounds during the attempts to add "singing" to the ritual. The effect is quite the contrary to what was intended: instead of creating an elevated state of the soul and mind, there is uncomfortable uneasiness and confusion.

Some lodges just play a piece of music by the "organist" (even if recorded), followed by a silent period of contemplation and self-examination, after which they continue the ritual.

There is a young composer in Florida who composed music for every step of each degree in their ("American") ritual. In an affinity lodge with musician members, the singing is uplifting. The possibilities are endless… both for success and failure.

What kind of music would *your* lodge need?

32 INTERNAL VERSUS EXTERNAL

Normally, the reference to the phrase comes up nowadays only when a dress code is discussed, and more often than not, it is used as an excuse for sloppy menswear in the lodges. (Reminder: *"The internal, and not the external, qualifications of a man, are what masonry regards."* – it is a quote from William Preston's *Illustration of Masonry*, 1796.)

However, it is worth noting that the original text mentions "external qualifications" which people then project on the [external] *look*! The keyword is: *qualifications*. As so often, we need to clarify first what the phrase meant for people in the 18th century when it was first published in the well-known text by William Preston.

First, let us take a look at the external qualifications that were considered in the British Empire of the time, for example, when appointing someone for an office in the courts or in administration. It was never about aptitudes, skills, or merit… but birth-right (nobility) and social status, wealth, and connections. Eventually, some education. None of them refers to the *character* of the person. None of them were concerned with the real internal traits: is he a good person, is he an honest, upright man?

And those are the traits, the character traits that Masonry is looking for in a man. One of the most quoted slogans in the Craft is "we take good men and make them better". Most people cannot grasp even such a simple sentence, where the emphasis is – or should be – on the *good*. Good before he even knocks on the door. We cannot take any man and try to "educate" him into something *better*. We are not the John Howard Society helping criminals to rebuild their lives. (N.B.: That society does a wonderful job – but it is not our mandate!)

My villager grandpa on Sunday mornings in the summertime shaved himself standing on the porch, then washed his upper body standing in the sunshine in the yard, and grandma brought him from the "nice room" a clean white shirt. They had to leave by the time the third bell had rung or they were late for the service. As grandpa was preparing his mind and soul to be ready for the sermon, he considered it necessary to prepare his "external" (body), too. In honour of the sacred, in respect for his fellow church members, and most importantly, to mirror his elevated, cleansed soul which was ready to absorb the Word.

Yet, there are Masons who think they must defend the casual attire of those that enter the sacred temple of Masonry in boots full of cattle manure... Sometimes literally, sometimes "allegorically" we enter the Temple of the lodge room with dirty shoes. Which is a reflection of the soul and mind that wasn't cleansed before, not being ready to share the Masonic experience.

Once a Mason told me that since the moment he placed a Square & Compasses decal on his car, he became a more polite driver, stopped showing the middle finger to fellow drivers and obeyed the rules of traffic.

It is true that society became less focused on dress code, the casual is the norm almost everywhere. But it was also observed that men behave differently if they are dressed up in a more festive manner... So, maybe there is a relationship between how we dress and how we behave.

Your dress code?

33 HOW MANY IS TOO MANY

There are places with one Grand Lodge. Others with two. And others with over fifty…

It happens more often than we like to think and in more places than we would want. When a place, a geographical region, is close to our heart; when we like it, we would like to see it as the perfect place in every regard, as a place that doesn't have anything embarrassing. But real life, even Masonic life, sometimes leaves us embarrassed. Take the case of the number of grand lodges (and here it is used deliberately without capital letters).

The so-called American Doctrine established exclusive jurisdictional rules to the effect that there can be only one Grand Lodge in a state. It also means that no other Grand Lodge is allowed to "invade" that territory… and when this doctrine had spread worldwide, invading many countries around the globe, it became so revered that many Masons started to consider it a "landmark". Just to clarify it: it is not a landmark[16]… Beyond the American Doctrine, we can consider it a time honoured tradition around the world. Of course, history, and peculiar

---

[16] This book discusses landmarks in another chapter.

developments in Masonry of some territories, resulted in more complicated situations than any Masonic theoretician could come up with.

Let's start with "America" itself. For about 200 years the exclusivism was well and alive, until the expectations of the present era pressured (almost all) American Grand Lodges to acknowledge and recognize their Prince Hall counterpart Grand Lodges, de facto sanctioning the end of the exclusive jurisdictional rule – although only for these two Grand Lodges in a state. The Prince Hall Grand Lodges have a research website, and they organized a committee years ago that goes today by the name of the Phylaxis Society's Commission on Bogus Masonic Practices. According to their research, some states have two or three such "bogus" bodies, while others have a long list of tens and tens of such self-styled "grand lodges".

If we were to look only at the American landscape of bogus Masonry, we would be inclined to see it as a phenomenon affecting especially the Black communities. However, before we draw such conclusions, we need to look into the recent (Masonic) history of the Eastern European countries, where we could easily find the same number of irregular and competing "grand bodies" as in some American states plagued by this unfortunate development.

Even in more stable places like Western Europe, we can bring up the example of Italy, in which case the United Grand Lodge of England (UGLE) and the majority of the United States Grand Lodges recognize different Grand Lodges; or France, where they also have at least a dozen grand lodges – some recognized and some not. (And sometimes it is difficult to differentiate because the "external" difference might be one small word in their name...)

The most important question that comes up when discussing the subject is the reason for such a proliferation of "grand lodges" and other similar organizations. All the reasons can easily be listed under one of these two motives: money and ego. The so called grand lodges are either started by conmen with the intent to get enormous amounts of money for "initiation" and membership from the gullible candidates, or by individuals with a despicable character trait, an inflated ego that responds to any possible conflict situation with the irresistible urge to form their own "grand lodge" where they can dictate and lead. Even with an unhappy group (and not an offended individual) which splits from the established body to form a new entity, in addition to the concerns of a Masonic nature, there are strong egos driving the secession. Such Masonic concerns could be the disregard for the landmarks, innovations, deviations from the traditional practices, etc.

So, is there an ideal number of grand bodies in a jurisdiction? Everyone probably has a different answer to this. Based on some European examples, it seems that the most harmonious Masonic life and activity happens in places having a regular (UGLE-recognized) Grand Lodge, another Grand Lodge that is of the "French" (continental, adogmatic, irregular) orientation, usually recognized by the Grand Orient(s), a mixed Droit Humain type grand body, and women-only lodges. That should be enough. Or, maybe another one for Masons who are unhappy with the status quo.

Can we accept that Masonry comes in many flavours and colours?

34 ON MASONIC PHILOSOPHY

How many times do we hear the phrase *Masonic philosophy*, or the philosophy of Freemasonry, our philosophy, our basic tenets, and so on? Let's take a closer look. Does Freemasonry have some specific philosophy that sets it apart from other similar schools of thought? Is it possible to define a specific philosophical theory that is exclusive to Freemasonry?

If we look into the theoretical-philosophical sources of how Freemasonry describes the world, interprets the world around us, and man's place in it, we may get disoriented. Of course, the man in this case being a Freemason, we talk about our place in the world, in the universe, in the creation of the supreme architect of the universe. The confusion comes from the fact that it is nearly impossible to restrict the trends to one single source.

When perusing the writings of different Masonic authors who analyzed this question, their works often refer us to many different sources. It's a wide range from unconventional Christian sects, like the early Gnostics to ancient Greek philosophers, like the Stoics, and the later Hellenistic schools, mainly Neoplatonism (which was, in a simplistic definition, a reinterpretation of Plato's philosophy).

All these were influences that can be discovered by looking into all the layers of our Masonic texts. Finally, the influence of the early Renaissance Neoplatonists, namely Marsilio Ficino and Giovanni Pico della Mirandola. (The latter wrote the famous essay *Oration on the Dignity of Man*.) These two names were also connected with the hermetic revival in the Western Renaissance – and looking back on the whole spectrum of philosophical strands, it is easy to understand the very divergent results as contemporary Masons try to reveal (or at least to trace) the great richness of the philosophical traditions embedded in the Masonic rituals.

And when all these ideas, together with the Alchemical teachings of the old continent, arrived in the British Islands, this resulted in a novel approach, arching from the Baconian school and method to Newton's philosophy, laying the foundations for modern science.

Looking for the intellectual foundation of Freemasonry, more specifically of what we call Masonic philosophy, is a challenging task for every theoretically inclined Mason. Sometimes it seems even more difficult to accept the multitude of originating ideas and the sometimes competing philosophies, without adhering to one single current, while discarding everything else.

The danger of limiting our interpretation of Freemasonry to one single possible philosophical foundation is that using a singular point of view it will distort our understanding of the intertwined traditions. In other words: restricting a person's interpretation to one single prism of one singular philosophical school, may lead to a twisted understanding of the original intent.

Even just a superficial overview of the philosophical trends which are clearly identifiable in our texts and teachings, reveals a plethora of schools and traditions, all of them enriching our journey as we progress in Masonry.

It could be a fascinating undertaking to write a book

about all the philosophical sources of the worldview projected in our Masonic rituals.

Which source is closest to your understanding?

35 THE DOUBLE HERITAGE

We know by now that our rituals and ceremonial texts (lectures, explanations etc.) have multiple sources. Parts of them originating quite apart in time, in different periods of history.

Some of our initial ritualistic fragments that survived till today clearly show strong Christian overtones with obvious early Renaissance and subsequent Rosicrucian influences. Think of the ubiquitous references to the Saints John (removed by the 1813 Union), the emphasis on the art of memory in Schaw's statutes, and the early esoteric references to the "universal reformation of mankind" – all these can be traced in the Masonic lore, if we carefully read our texts.

The second half of the 1700s, with the Enlightenment in full swing, brought another very important contribution to the development of our philosophy, especially in the continental Freemasonry of the era. With this latter trend, Freemasonry became a very complex philosophical-ideological construct. There was, and still exists, an esoteric, more occult component of our symbolism and our teachings. At the same time, there is this rational, intellectual heritage of "natural philosophy", of emerging scientific research and a worldview – especially on the old continent of Europe, combined with some basic human rights issues. (Interestingly, these ideals of liberty later will become more prominent in the Scottish Rite degrees, which refer to them *expressis verbis* during the degrees; those originated in France but got the present elaborate form in the USA…)

Of course, the above summary is a very simplistic way of looking at the history of the Craft and its ceremonial texts, but it can serve as a starting point to develop an understanding of the *dual character* of our intellectual-spiritual heritage. It may help to explain why one Mason thinks of his journey through the degrees as an esoteric advancement in knowledge and understanding, while another fellow Craftsman identifies himself with the "natural philosophy" of science and nature. Quite often we can witness a bitter argument between the representatives of these two "hidden trends", both claiming exclusive rights to define the essence of Freemasonry for all.

In a way, both Masons are right: what they perceive is there in the ritual(s) and lectures. Most likely, their personalities resonate to different vibes, different sublime messages, so they "see" only one half of the whole pie. However, they would both be wrong if they were trying to push everybody else to accept their interpretation.

A well-rounded Mason would strive to learn not only a partial view, a simplistic narrow interpretation, like driving on a one-way street, but the whole complexity of the embedded teachings. He should open both his heart and his mind to grasp, feel, and live what Freemasonry is. Or, to continue the driving image from the previous sentence, let's drive on a wide highway up to the top of the mountain from where one can see the horizon in every direction, like from the centre of a circle…

Personally, I tend to favour those rational teachings that challenge my intellect. Patient brothers encourage me to embrace the more esoteric aspects, too. Where do you stand on this?

36 ON HEROES & EDUCATION

For more than two centuries one of the legendary Masonic hero role models was **John Coustos,** a native of Switzerland, but "naturalized" Englishman and Mason, who went to France and then to Portugal, organized a lodge and as a consequence, was arrested by the Portuguese Inquisition in 1743. After almost two years spent in prison he was released, went home, and in 1746 he published a book about his sufferings. He claimed that he never ever broke his Masonic obligation of secrecy, even when cruelly tortured by the Inquisition. That's why he became a hero. And for over 200 years, he was this legendary figure of the secretive Freemason, who kept our secrets, etc.

Then in the 1960s they opened the archives of the Portuguese Inquisition, and researchers found the very detailed minutes, records of his confessions: he told, actually, everything he knew, his confession is a very detailed early description of the ritual(s) used in his lodges from England, France, and Portugal… moreover, it contains one of the earliest references to of some elements today found only in the Royal Arch degree. Actually, I found this info when I was researching early sources of the

Royal Arch degrees and ritual.

The records were also translated into English, and the most renowned Masonic researcher and author from Ontario, **Wallace McLeod** published them in the prestigious Masonic Book Club series[17], with an introductory study. His findings and analysis of the original were also published in the proceedings of the world's premier research lodge, Quatuor Coronati[18].

Did this discovery change the prevailing "lore" of Masons about the true story of John Coustos? Not really.

And this brings us to an interesting anomaly – since we are talking not only about heroes but also about education. Even after having irrefutable proof that our hero was lying in his book, because under torture he revealed everything he knew about the Craft and the ritual, the poor man still maintains his hero status. (As of late some scholars alleged that even in his London mother lodge he was a spy for the Hanoverian-Whig establishment… but that's a different story.)

Of course, it is understandable that just like all humans, Masons also prefer romantic, inspiring stories – legends, if you will – instead of cold and sometimes uncomfortable truths. The legends, the mythological stories always are well-rounded and have a happy ending, and their morale is to stick to the values inculcated in our ritual, and at the end the world we will reward us.

We all need inspiring stories. Just as our rituals are not factual "history" of the ancient builders, but parables to convey a message (remember: *Freemasonry is a beautiful system* etc. etc.). Similarly, the legends about the Craft and especially its early period are not actual history.

---

[17] Coustos, John, *The Sufferings of John Coustos* with an introduction Wallace McLeod, (Bloomington: The Masonic Book Club, 1979).

[18] McLeod, Wallace, 'John Coustos: His lodges and his book', *AQC*, vol. 92 (1979).

Unfortunately, they were – and still are – handed down to the next generations of Craftsmen, without warning them of the fictional character of the stories. As today's media would say: we feed them fake information.

As often happens, real life can have a more adventurous aspect than the fictional stories we push as history. John Coustos was not the spotless character he tried to present himself to be – although we should not condemn his behaviour until we know how we would behave in the torture chambers of the Inquisition. But he inadvertently became one of the earliest sources of rituals used in the early period of Freemasonry.

Maybe we could use that late discovery as veritable educational material in our lodges.

37 ADMONITIONS OF SZENT ISTVÁN

My namesake, better to say, the first Hungarian king after whom I was named (although I was told that I inherited my father's name), and who, around 1000 A.D, forcibly Christianized the migratory tribes settled in Pannonia – Saint Stephen or Szent István, ruled for decades and he was hoping that his only son, Imre (Emeric) would continue his work. In order to help his heir, he "wrote" Admonitions to his son, containing guidelines for having a successful reign. (The quotation marks around the word *wrote* refer to the fact that most likely he was illiterate, just as most of the kings around Europe in his time, and the manuscript was actually written by a learned contemporary clergyman.)

Although his hopeful heir, Emeric/Imre (also a saint in his own right in the Catholic calendar) died young, the Admonitions survived the centuries and certain passages were often quoted to us while we went through our school years. One of those lines is immensely powerful: "***For a kingdom of one tongue, or of one custom, is weak and fragile.***" A teaching mostly neglected by all the nationalistic leaders who built their propaganda on exactly the opposite ideas of one nation, one language, one empire, one leader…

Does that admonition have any relevance for Masons of the 21st century in North America? Or anywhere else, in the Masonic world? Before attempting to answer that question, let me approach it from a different angle. How many languages (*tongues*) are allowed in your Masonic jurisdiction? How many rituals (*customs*) are permitted to be used in the lodges under your grand lodge? And a personal one: how many languages can you read?

I am always confused by the simple fact that my mother jurisdiction, in a quasi-monolingual landlocked country in the middle of Europe allows four languages and many different rituals in their lodges, while my present jurisdiction in the centre of a land of *immigrants* is obsessively monolingual and mono-ritualistic (we just made up this last word, but everyone should understand it)! Even elsewhere in Canada (or the USA) other jurisdictions were and are more generous toward their newcomers, allowing them to work in their own mother tongue.

However, that is only one side of the "kingdom of one tongue." More concerning should be that if we look at the citations and bibliographies accompanying the average research papers written in English in our jurisdictions, the language horizon is very narrow: English and nothing else. Considering that both German and French Freemasonry have published extraordinary works and research in this field, the systemic neglect of the rich literature accumulated in those languages looks like an inexplicable anomaly. Of course, in our era, when due to online communications English has become the *lingua franca*[19] of the world, asking English speakers to learn other languages

---

[19] Literally: the language of the Franks; it was a French/Italian based jargon developed by Crusaders and traders spoken in early Middle Ages in Levant among speakers of the many vernaculars that were not mutually intelligible.

would be counterproductive or in vain. That's a trend, a worldwide trend which seems unstoppable nowadays.

Side note about the *lingua franca*: although originally it referred to one specific "pidgin" of the Eastern Mediterranean region, later every language having similar functions got labelled the same. One can say that Aramaic had been used in that way before the Crusaders' time; or classical Latin was the "lingua franca" of European scholars for long centuries; during the Enlightenment period French became the language of international diplomacy (and of playful flirting), and later on, in Mitteleuropa – Central Europe – German was the language of scientific publishing at the height of the German Empire and the Austro-Hungarian Monarchy in that region.

Even if all that non-English knowledge is now buried in distant libraries of academic institutions or grand lodges of regular and irregular Masonic bodies, publishers, and Masonic publications of today could and should keep a finger on the pulse of Masonic research in other languages. If for nothing else, to get a refreshing new perspective on everything we think we know. We may realize that some of those platitudes that are often brought up in our Masonic discussions are incorrect or simply not true. But unfortunately, for many years, one can barely find a translation of a scholarly Masonic work from French or German. Or Spanish or Italian...

I emphasized the German-language Masonic literature of the 19-20th century and the same French literature of the 20-21st century because they represent a huge corpus of extraordinary works: making available previously unpublished sources, revealing historical facts, explaining the development of the many rituals, etc.

One can, of course, guess why Anglo-American Freemasonry is not paying attention to anything written in other languages. Maybe we are just following the general trend of scientific literature – whoever is not published and/or cited in English… practically doesn't exist.

It could be that some authors or respectable research libraries belong to grand bodies that we deem "irregular".

Or just different enough to keep them away from our little world of mundane preoccupations filled with routine.

Can we name at least one contemporary non-English Masonic author?

38 CONCERNING GOD AND RELIGION - TODAY

In regular Masonry we require belief in a Supreme Being from our candidates. The emphasis here is on the word *being* (as in a person or thing that exists). We can occasionally hear well-intentioned Masons saying that it can be any "superior power" – but power is not necessarily a being. From a theological or philosophical point of view that requirement referring to a being is a **theist** approach.

Most of the time Freemasons don't spend too much time on theological nuances, however the restriction forbidding "quarrels about religion" (as Anderson put it 300 years ago, in 1723[20]) shouldn't prevent us even from philosophical clarifications of our own expectations or principles. The only terminology we remember from the Old Charges is the "atheist", which we also label "stupid"… And if atheists are stupid, we, the believers in that Supreme Being, are smart and clever. The good guys. Simplistic logic works like a charm – even for Freemasons.

---

[20] It is worth noting that in 1738, in the next edition of the Constitution the text has been placed under different heading.

However, certain distinctions in terminology are important, not only for philosophers, but for ordinary people, too. Especially for Masons, since we get selective and even exclusionist based on the theological aspects of the belief system of our candidates. Let's give it a try: both *theists* and *deists* do believe in a Supreme Being, though they have a different conception regarding the role of that deity in man's life. Seemingly, it's only a difference of a few letters, TH vs. D – but the consequences are huge. (For lovers of words: at the beginning both words meant the same, they were used interchangeably, but by the late 1600s the meanings started to take a divergent path.)

Question: does the requirement in our Craft tell the candidate to be a theist, or do you think he can be a deist as well? We may need here a reminder that for people in the 1700s, and even today, a deist was someone who believed that the Creator Being (Supreme Creator?) created this world, the universe, or whatever they imagined the "world" would be, and after that left it on its own, without interfering in the everyday lives of humans. It was a mechanistic view, considering the complexity of the issue, but for those times, it was adequate. Some cosmological writings referred to this idea as the Big Watchmaker who set up the mechanism, and now the mechanism is working forever. In this mechanical universe, the Creator doesn't have to be present in each person's life to regulate their actions… Strictly speaking, deists were/are also monotheists, i.e. believing in one single god, although not necessarily the God of the Bible. In their worldview, in this universe created and left on its own, man's *free will* occupied a central place. (However, in the Old Charges of the Antients' Constitution from 1751, they mention deists, and exclude them from the Craft.)

Before we attempt to deal with the characteristics of a theist in the Masonic context, we need to briefly clarify two related categories, which define men (and women, of course) outside of this dichotomy. Both are composed with the Old Greek negative prefix **a-**, also known by its scientific name of *"alpha privative"*. Its most common meaning in English is non- or un- or without... The two words to look at are agnostic and atheist. *Gnosis* meant knowledge in Greek, but with this prefix today's meaning is "impossible to know" – and we use it to describe individuals who think they cannot declare themselves believing or not believing in a deity, for the simple fact that faith is not knowledge, and besides faith they don't see any evidence for the existence of such a deity. Consequently, they sit on the fence, so to speak, in this discussion. They are *agnostics*. On the other hand, we have the dreaded (stupid[21]) *atheist* – a person who explicitly denies the existence of any kind of deity, no matter what it is called.

We were told in the early moments how to deal with these atheist guys: since they don't understand the Art (Freemasonry was called the "Royal Art") – they are kept out. But it seems to be trickier with the guys on the fence: originally, the word meant an opinion as for the *unknowability of nature*. But later got this narrower interpretation of skepticism toward religion and, more importantly, rejection of Christian beliefs. That's where it gets murky for the contemporary Masons: what if the candidate answers that he doesn't know the answers to our questions?

And we didn't even mention yet the *polytheists*...

---

[21] They were labeled as such in the early Masonic Constitutions.

39 IS THIS A THEATRE PLAY?

Most Masons would be upset if we say that the ceremony of the rituals is similar to a role play, although for outsiders it would resemble a theatre performance. But do we have a reason to be upset by such a comparison? Or should we look into it with an open mind? Let's consider the following quote, which explains the connection between theatre and ritual:

"Anthropologists and historians have long believed that Western theater originated from religious rituals, such as the Egyptian cult of Osiris and the City Dionysia festivals of ancient Greece. Contemporary scholars of performance place theater and ritual on a continuum of *rehearsed human behaviours* that permeate social life and persist into the 21st century."[22] – *emphasis added.*

Personally, I might be biased because at the beginning

---

[22] Pannill Camp, Ph.D. Assistant Professor of drama at Washington University in St. Louis, studies performance theory, theatre architecture, Freemasonry and theatre of ritual, and the history of modern western theatre, in particular exchanges between theatre and philosophy in seventeenth and eighteenth-century France. (see Bibliography)

of my career as journalist I used to write theatre critiques and before that, during my university years, I participated in a student theatre group, as an actor and director. No wonder I find the art of theatre one of the most impactful artistic endeavours and achievements of mankind. And in our Masonic landscape, groups that perform flawless degree work, and go around their jurisdiction and beyond to present such rehearsed "shows", are basically "Masonic theatre performers" at their best. And conversely, when we sit in a lodge room where none of the players know their role (text and choreography) and the candidate has to hear every line twice, once from the prompter and next from the member trying to do his part, quite often we feel some sort of embarrassment for the "players" who so miserably underperform in the ritual. N.B.: I used to have this uncomfortable "feeling bad for them" feeling even in a real theatre if a troupe was not at its best…

If we study any kind of ritual known to mankind across the globe, there are always strong **theatrical elements** in them. There are actors/players who perform their memorized parts (*text, often sacred text in oral traditions*), there is a certain choreography (well-practised *ritualistic movements in space: steps*), there are other members of the group watching them (*spectators*), there even could be music or songs and, eventually, a symbolic alternation of lights and darkness. All of these can be also observed during the conferral of degrees in the Masonic rituals.

Anybody having a basic knowledge of theatre is aware that the "end result" that we see and enjoy when the curtain goes up on the opening night, was realized by endless rehearsals and practice, individually and in a team, to create that wonderful illusion which will mesmerize those present. Do we, Masonic players, mesmerize our new candidates on the night of initiation?

Most Masons are not actors, or not such talented actors. Although those familiar with the Ancient &

Accepted Scottish Rite[23] (AASR) ceremonies performed usually twice a year while conferring their degrees can attest to the theatrical character of those events. Actually, some of the buildings where the rituals and their "illustrations" happen have a real stage with professional decor, lighting, and costumes for the "players". These scenes are not performed by outsider actors but by the AASR-members volunteering to create the proper experience for the candidates watching the "show".

In the Craft lodges (also called Blue lodges or symbolic lodges) the division between players and spectators is not always as obvious. Members can switch between being active performers in a part and then going back to being spectators. But it's still a team effort, having the Master of the lodge as the director and conductor coordinating the roles and the performance.

Some might fear to compare the ritual's role play to theatre, mainly because in the public sphere we also have derogatory connotations attached to it, e.g. "political theatre" which denotes the general dissatisfaction with the behaviour of policymakers. However, in the Masonic context, the idea of theatre alludes to the more ancient human traditions of "rehearsed human behaviour" aimed to cause awe and elation in all participants.

How is your theatre performing?

---

[23] One of the so-called appendant bodies of Freemasonry, offering the "high grades". In this volume we deliberately don't discuss topics pertaining the appendant bodies unless it is inevitable to mention them.

40 DEMOCRACY INCUBATORS?

When a while ago, on an airplane, I read a debate focusing on why millennials are many times more dissatisfied with the democratic system (than people were in 1940, for example), I dismissed it as we do with sensationalistic articles. Allegedly, in the 1940s, liberal democracy was supported because it made people wealthier. But millennials think that's not true anymore.

However, several issues that came up in that discussion examining the "democratic crisis" echoed different concerns: lack of civic engagement, lack of civic participation in small local organizations that used to be considered the learning playgrounds of democracy. Also, they claimed that universities and colleges shifted the focus from the **core civic values** serving a democratic free world to more hyped topics (which are not of our concern right now).

The concern might be the *democratic deficiency* witnessed in many places around the world. Can Freemasonry offer a solution to address the need? Maybe.

When we talk about the early period of Freemasonry, we often mention proudly that certain basic ideas of *modern democracy* have been introduced and practiced first in the

Masonic lodges from where they've spread to the society at large. And it would be a logical step to think that if no organization is offering the basic teaching and instilling the values of a democratic free world... we might have a chance to make the lodges again the incubators of the "democratic experiment" as our forefathers used to do at the dawn of the modern era.

Next question, if we indeed have this unique chance in our time: Are we prepared to fulfil this role? It's a noble ideal, but it could be more difficult to achieve than we think. The chief obstacle becomes obvious if we look at the social composition of the membership of the lodges: it is very rare to have *decision makers* among them. I use the term as a broad category, while trying to avoid references to (the higher or lower) socioeconomic status of the members. The "decision maker" is a leader position in a democracy where anyone can arrive *by merit only* in an array of activities: political on every level of government, economic, cultural, military, etc. Unfortunately, in the past several decades, very few decision makers on any level joined the lodges. As a consequence, our noble ideas inculcated in the moral lessons of the degrees cannot permeate the society. Then what else is there to be done?

If all the other existing institutions gave up on teaching democratic and civic values, stopped functioning as the breeding ground for leaders, stopped preparing the future leadership of the country – let's make the lodges again into such places where all this can happen!

The key component in this plan should be to attract young, educated, smart men! Transform the lodges into highly intellectual laboratories. We might have a **historical chance,** just as our forefathers had in their time.[24]

---

[24] 20 years ago a book has been published by the noted Canadian author and Masonic scholar Wallace McLeod and the American Masonic author Allen. E. Roberts: *Freemasonry and Democracy: Its Evolution in North America.*

Each jurisdiction will have to find their own way to achieve this. Some places experiment with the so-called university scheme, attracting young students to lodges on and around the campus, others try to bring back more philosophical, intellectual discussions for the benefit of members. A few revisit the "proper vs. improper solicitation" debate and act according to their conclusions…

Or we just can continue to live in our fading ivory tower.

41 THE TEMPLE IN THE AIR

Ever since the founding of modern Freemasonry, the temple of King Solomon at Jerusalem played a particularly important role in the symbolism of the craft. However, it has nothing to do with the "origins" of the Craft.

It is important to pay attention to the word *symbolism* because what we have in the different ritualistic texts of the first three degrees in Freemasonry is not a literal history of the temple in Jerusalem. (Some archaeologists even argue that the temple described in the Old Testament might actually be fictional, meaning there might be a chance, according to them, that the temple did not exist.)

There was a 17th-century Moravian[25] theologian, teacher, scientist, author, and the father of modern pedagogy, who is buried in the Netherlands, in the city of Naarden. In Europe, his work and importance is taught almost everywhere in institutions where future teachers are trained. In the 1600s the trustees of Harvard planned to invite him to lead the new "school" there, but he wasn't able to take that position. His tomb and memorial is

---

[25] The land of Moravia today is the Eastern part of Czech Republic.

maintained by Masons—both from the Netherlands and Czechia, although we know for sure that he wasn't a Freemason. Then why?

His name is *Jan Amos Komenský*, also known as *Comenius*—a Latinized form of his name, as was customary in that era. He was a bishop of the Moravian Brethren, an early protestant church (founded before the Lutheran reformation) and one of the brightest minds of his time. Religious wars forced him and his congregation to go into exile, so he was "wandering" in Europe from the Netherlands to Poland, from England to Transylvania, from Sweden to Hungary…

Samuel Hartlieb (also: Hartlib) of the Invisible College fame, the great "intelligencer" of his time was instrumental in inviting Comenius to England in 1641. Before that, in 1636 Komenský wrote to him about his plans, a letter which was printed at Oxford University without the knowledge of the author. Komenský, while describing in this letter his plans to build a **Temple of Wisdom**, mentions *Wisdom, Strength, and Beauty* as threefold to God, Nature, and Art. In the third edition he introduced a well-known Masonic symbol ∴ the three dots in a triangle. Lots of questions…

Komenský's life would make an excellent adventure TV-show, and discussing his works would require a separate book. Here we should focus only on two details that somehow seem to be connected with Freemasonry. What Comenius and his English patrons contemplated has been recorded in the book **Via Lucis** (*The Way of Light*[26]), written in London in the winter of 1641-42 but published later. (In that year the civil war started, and Komenský had to leave London.) He planned an *international academy* with resident and corresponding members. In 1668, when he published his Via Lucis, he dedicated it "*to the torchbearers of*

---

[26] Light is often used in Freemasonry as the symbol of knowledge.

this enlightened age, members of the Royal Society of London, now bringing real philosophy to a happy birth." The Royal Society[27] is *de facto* the academy of science of England even today. A repository of knowledge, if you will, *Templum Sophiae*—Temple of Wisdom. As if his suggestions from over twenty years earlier finally materialized.

In a video lecture I explained that the idea of a "temple of wisdom" or as often referred to: a temple of knowledge, a repository of encyclopedic human knowledge was **in the air**[28] during the centuries before organized modern Freemasonry was established—and, quite obviously, Comenius' ideas were inspirational in founding such an institution. Since the humanist revival of the ancient lore and through the *Renaissance* (which means 'rebirth'—of the ancient arts and sciences) Jerusalem became a widely accepted symbol of the ideal city. Many utopian authors echoed in some shape this idea, and the Temple also came to symbolize the wisdom of its legendary builder—King Solomon—meanwhile being transformed into a perennial imaginary edifice where all human knowledge was stored for generations to come.

Thomas More, Tommaso Campanella, Johannes Valentinus Andreae, and Sir Francis Bacon are just a few names[29] that preceded Komenský and his description of such a Temple. On the cover of Bacon's utopian work, Masons can discover many recognizable visual symbols

---

[27] There are theories that link the Invisible College, the Royal Society and Freemasonry as an organic network in spreading the new ideas of the Enlightenment.

[28] See the playlist of presentations made for the VOOSA (Virtual Order of Sapere Aude) -
https://www.youtube.com/playlist?list=PL2goIWm-RQiMQnKhsQodY4JvH0jgBdoyz

[29] Such works were Thomas More: *Utopia* (1516), Tommaso Campanella: *Civitas Solis* (The City of the Sun, 1602) (*published later in 1623), Johannes Valentinus Andreae: *Christianopolis* (1616), and Sir Francis Bacon: *New Atlantis* (1627).

which support the idea that Freemasonry later borrowed lavishly from existing representations and narratives to fabricate its own legendarium.

In Komenský's writings, all these ideas are also present, which explains the choice of the epigraph at the front of this book. However, we have another reason why Comenius must be discussed here. And in the spirit of the topic, we "borrowed" this idea[30] from a Czech scholar—Josef Roucek—who lived most of his life in the USA. Roucek studied the original (Latin) texts and their Czech translations, and concluded:

> *"[o]ne of the least known historical facts in the field of the modern Masonic movement is that John Amos Comenius (Komenský), well known for his contributions to the rise of modern pedagogy (education), can be also credited for his original contributions to the formulation of its original ideology. To state our thesis briefly, the importance of Comenius to the whole Masonic movement can be appreciated from the fact that his general ideas served James Anderson to compile in 1717 the Statutes of Freemasonry." (Roucek 371)*

> *"James Anderson (together with John*

---

[30] Roucek, Josef S. "Jan Amos Komenský: The Spiritual Founder of Modern Masonic Mouvement." *Zeitschrift Für Religions- Und Geistesgeschichte*, vol. 15, no. 4, Brill, pp. 371–76, doi:10.2307/23894786. Accessed 15 July 2020.

Theophilus Desaguliers became the architects and authors of the movement known in history as the 'The Revival'. To Dr. Anderson was intrusted the duty of compiling the 'general records and faithful traditions from the beginning of time', and to enable his doing so all the available documents were collected for his use, [t]here were afterwards destroyed. That resulted in irreparable loss. In 1723 the 'New Constitutions' were published. This document which literally 'lifted' numerous passages from the works of Komenský, completely changed the theory of the institution - from Christian to the adoption of a universal creed based on the Fatherhood of God and the Brotherhood of Man - so as to admit men of all religions, nationalities, and stations in life." (Roucek 372)

This theory of Roucek that Anderson copied from Comenius, was not accepted in the Masonic literature. The reason could be that English-speaking scholars rarely read anything written in other languages, like German or Czech. On the other hand, a future researcher may prove it to be completely erroneous.

As I mentioned at the beginning, Dutch and Czech Freemasons take care of Komenský's memorial. What do they know that we don't?

42 THE LINGUISTIC ANALYSIS THAT NEVER HAPPENED*

Our rituals, probably well over a hundred of them, have one thing in common: they were memorized but never analyzed, they have been explained but never studied.

Let's clarify this by an analogy. The Holy Books[31] of the Bible, the Sacred Volume of Western civilization has been studied for centuries, and not only by theologians. Probably, beginning with Baruch Spinoza and through the burgeoning biblical scholarship of the late 19th century, up till our days the Bible has been studied by linguists, literary critics, historians, translators, even archaeologists and academics in the fields of mythology, history of ideas, folklore and so on.

But in the Masonic literature there is not any allusion or mention of any kind of linguistic (or literary/stylistic) study targeting the ritualistic texts of Freemasonry.

Cultural anthropology often describes the very complex

---

[31] *biblos* = book in Greek, pl. *biblia*
*A larger version of this text was presented at the 10th anniversary Symposium of the Hungarian Quatuor Coronati Circle, in 2022.

characteristics of a culture, likening it to an onion. First, we can see only the outer layer of the onion, then after removing it, there is another layer, under which there is another one… until we get to the innermost core of it. Actually, this metaphor can be applied to our linguistic analysis as well. All texts have many features which can be analyzed with the proper tools. Such research could reveal a richness of unimaginable proportions. It will reveal not only the primary meaning, but also the purpose and the intent of the author(s), the involuntarily embedded assumptions, worldviews, and cultural biases of the authors. All these are encoded in the language usage, the style, the literary tools employed by the authors.

It should be clarified that many books and articles have been written about the *history* of the rituals, trying to reconstruct its evolution from the first surviving documents and fragments, through the *aide-mémoires* disguised as "exposés" and real exposés (best known are the English and French ones from the 18th century). However, those works are not a substitute for the missing literary and linguistic analysis.

I am making comparisons with Bible studies mainly due to the fact that few other written texts have been analyzed more thoroughly, setting an example for the methodology and scientific approach that is desired for a deeper understanding of the rituals.

Understandably, there have been and still are inherent difficulties in making the ritualistic texts accessible for linguistic studies. The references to the language used in the written and printed rituals are very rare and, usually, they are limited to describing it as solemn, "archaic" or old, and difficult to memorize. This is not enough for a linguistic or stylistic analysis.

In the English-speaking world, one of the most recognizable and widely used rituals is the Emulation (together with all the derivates from it). The other would be the "American Ritual" as the Preston-Webb ritual is known to many. Some version of the latter one is used in all USA jurisdictions, except Pennsylvania. Despite the very significant differences between *Emulation* and *Preston-Webb*, a closer look would reveal that both have common sources. Revealing and identifying all the common sources in the ritualistic texts would once again remind us of the methods used by biblical scholars, who employ *textual criticism, source criticism, form criticism*, and *redaction criticism* together.

We need to remind ourselves that these methods are used in a much wider context than biblical studies. These are branches of philology developed for a more thorough understanding of the linguistic layers of any text.

Probably, the most prolific approach in the case of the ritualistic texts could be the combination of the two critical methods known as **form criticism** and **redaction criticism**. While the former is concerned with the – smaller – text "units" that usually take shape in the process of oral transmission of a tradition, the latter examines how the different sources and texts get edited into one single "document". Referring to the ritual fragments found in the early exposés that are recognizable in the present versions of rituals should be sufficient proof for the usefulness of such an endeavour.

In a similar vein, the **literary and stylistic analysis** would enhance our understanding of the authors' intent. Relating to the different periods of British literature, such a comparative work should look at the stylistic characteristics of the periods when the rituals were compiled; from the Restoration through the Augustan Age and until the Romanticism of the early 1800s, with possible influences of the Victorian era's prose in the final forms. Like the linguistic analysis, the stylistic approach could also be diversified depending on the focus.

Let's look at this issue in this context: here is a missed opportunity to go beyond the habitual moralistic interpretations of our rituals, using the well-established methodology for an analysis that is still waiting to happen. How would this help your understanding?

43 THE MISSED SYMBOLISM

A friend of mine, an excellent Transylvanian linguist and cultural anthropology professor teaches in one of his courses that we have – or at least used to have – a *double-layered language*. (Unfortunately, he teaches and writes only in Hungarian, so I can't recommend his work to English readers... unless you are ready to learn Hungarian[32].)

As he explains it, the double-layered in this case means that there is a more ancient, deeper layer that can be described as "symbolic" – a linguistic behaviour that relies on impressional representation of feeling and/or mood, which we understand inherently, without ever being taught. In his view, the linguistic model is the metaphorical organizing principle of how through using language the speaker of the language "acquires" the world, as opposed to the cognitive model that is a learned (taught?) layer of linguistic behaviour, displaying emotional neutrality – a rational model prevalent in scientific and academic texts.

---

[32] Prof. Szilágyi N. Sándor. His series of lectures on anthropology and linguistics is available on YouTube: https://www.youtube.com/playlist?list=PLZuxUQx7notThiAXo3ykRuzadnmPd6feU (accessed 2023-07-16)

If you wonder why we are trying to introduce here a linguistic theory positing the model of double-layered language, here is the answer. Any initiatic process is inherently symbolic behaviour, and even the spoken language in it belongs to the symbolic layer as described above. The Masonic initiation resembles the rites of passage model. In the 18th century, for example, it was customary to get a new name used in the Craft; the drama of the third degree is a rebirth (but definitely not resurrection as the ignorant fundamentalist critics believe!), i.e. a new stage of life; Masonic literature often compares the journey through the degrees with the progression of man through the vital cycles from youth to old age and death...

In the outside world, where similar initiatic ceremonies and rites still exist, the initiate actually has to experience the events, has to immerse themselves into the process, physically and mentally. They are not passive objects of the ceremony, but active subjects. Active participants.

The big paradox of our Masonic initiation is that while we try to mimic the initiatic ritual of rites of passage, we do not require the physical-mental-spiritual participation of the candidate. We tell them about the story without guiding them to live it and pass through it. And while we are talking to them, we rely mainly on the cognitive layer of language. On that cognitive layer which is void of emotions and symbolic elements, talking to the rational-intellectual cognitive parts of his brain.

From this point of view, only two archaic elements could be interpreted as real symbolic experiences during the initiation. One is still in use without understanding its importance (disrobing and divesting metals), while the other is making a timid attempt to be integrated in the practice of the observant lodges: the Chamber of Reflection.

However, the Chamber of Reflection is not popular even as an idea; it is rarely used because many North

American Masons perceive it as "foreign" from their traditions. This might be true, but it should be part of the process, as described in a seminal work in this field *"[r]ites of passage normally include a period in which the individual is alienated from the social structure…"*[33]

There is anecdotal evidence that the actors who participate in the role play (a.k.a. the degree team performing the initiation) often comment on the event mentioning that the whole thing "went over his head" – referring to the inability of the candidate to grasp the ceremony of the rite of passage meant to be on the participatory symbolic layer of the language.

How can Freemasonry convey a purely symbolic message using a rationalistic layer of language?

---

[33] Meletinsky, E. M. (2014, January 21). *Poetics of Myth*. Routledge. p.204

44 ON SPIRITUALITY

Ever since man (meaning: homo sapiens) became capable of self-reflection and of contemplation regarding his place in our ever expanding universe, some kind of "spiritual longing" began budding in his soul, or mind, or heart – depending on your views and beliefs.

If you look up "spirituality" in dictionaries to clarify its meaning, you can find as many definitions as there are dictionaries, although they all have something in common: the reference to the awareness of the feeling of the cosmic or divine nature of belonging. For millennia, this *spiritual need* was served well by the many religions of the world.

As a side note: if we try to trace the original Latin word – **spiritus** – which had the meaning of *breathing* or (obviously) *spirit*… how it fared in the different languages, we would be amazed to discover that from the holy ghost to alcohol many divergent meanings can occur.

In Freemasonry, it became a truism to refer to the "spiritual" aspects of the Craft, the spiritual needs of men, and similar topics. Sometimes even mixed up with esoteric aspects. But it is more lip service than actual involvement. Attending a regular or stated meeting in the lodges on this continent hardly ever has the effect of a "mind-altering" spiritual experience. Boredom cannot be accepted as a spiritual path…

The results of research a few years ago showed that an increasing number of people define themselves as "spiritual but not religious." Both in Canada and the USA this trend is lead by millennials, and we don't seem to pay attention to it[34]. Freemasonry comfortably skips the question, assuming that all the spiritual needs are satisfied by the religious affiliation of its members – practically, "delegating" the task of fulfilling the spiritual needs to the different churches.

Looking at the graphs illustrating this trend of increased spirituality, no Mason can avoid thinking of the question: can we admit candidates who declare themselves spiritual but not religious? Or is a bigoted zealous fundamentalist (of any religion or denomination) better than a deeply spiritual good guy, who is not religious? That's one question to think about…

Next, we should really ponder the spirituality we offer in the lodge. If any… How do we create an ambience and atmosphere that would instill some kind of spiritual elevation? The *spiritual longing* is still there, the question is how we respond to it. How is your lodge handling this issue?

Lastly, somewhat related to the starting point: what will we do in the long term when the overwhelming majority of our population will not be religious, "just" spiritual? Is the Craft ready? Are you ready?

---

[34] England and Wales, the jurisdiction of the UGLE which imposed on the Masonic world the requirement of the belief in a Supreme Being, doesn't fare better. According to the 2021 census less than half of the population (46.2%, 27.5 million people) described themselves as "Christian", a 13.1 percentage point decrease in 2011; despite this decrease, "Christian" remained the most common response to the religion question. "No religion" was the second most common response, increasing by 12.0 percentage points to 37.2% (22.2 million) from 25.2% (14.1 million) in 2011.

45 WHOSE SYMBOL IT IS ANYWAY?

There is a famous mosaic from Pompeii (today on display in the archaeological museum in Naples, Italy) that is known by its title "Memento mori". It is full of familiar images for Masons: plumb rule, square, skull... and some less familiar ones because they are not used in our narratives and symbolism. But the artwork (which it is) as a whole is a powerful representation of the well-known notion of our own mortality. Because *memento mori* means just that – a reminder of death, a reminder of our own mortality. Some people are scared of it, but we, as diligent students of the Craft, have learned to look at it in a philosophical manner and contemplate our lives in this way.

Far away from this example, on the Orkney Islands in the north of Scotland, tourists can visit St Magnus Cathedral in Kirkwall. Inside it, on the lower part of the walls of both aisles there are fascinating tombstones (they were lifted from the floor in the 19th century during renovation and inserted in the walls). Masons familiar with the concept of the Chamber of Reflection would be shocked to discover several objects used in those chambers carved in the late 1600s on the tombstone of an ordinary merchant from this town. Again, skulls, bones, candles...

These two examples should be sufficient to demonstrate that time and distance don't matter: the human mind displays its universality by using the same symbols to express the same ideas. Death? – Hamlet talks to a skull, and the spectators learn that Yorick (whose skull Hamlet holds in his hands) is gone and everything that made him the person known by his friends, gone, too: his lips are gone (not visible on the skull) and with it his jokes, his songs, his words are also gone. From the ancient Roman catacombs, full of human bones, to the international sign of 'mortal danger' showing a skull with two crossed bones, the message is the same. Memento mori.

Of course, some details may differ in a significant manner, and even more importantly, the interpretation of the details of the whole may vary culturally or historically, but the main message strikes the citizen of Pompeii and the new candidate in your lodge in the same way. Although, and that's the main message this week, the man in Pompeii and tomorrow's candidate in our lodge have nothing to do with each other. While it seems obvious, we need to emphasize this lack of connectedness, so here goes once more: there is no connection between the Roman citizens of Pompeii and today's Freemasons.

More often than not, when we see a "Masonic" symbol, we like to extrapolate and assume that even in that remote point in time or space, somebody was or is a Freemason. This way of thinking causes us more problems than we ever wanted to deal with. This mental trap is the result of the general lack of familiarity with ancient symbols. And our brain works in ways that often lead us to the wrong conclusions. Consider this example: if one event happens after another event, we connect them in a cause—effect relationship, meaning that we will see the first event as the cause of the following one, even if there is only sequential (time) relation.

Similarly, if we are familiar with a symbol, a certain image, or a phrase from the lodge, from our ritual, then encountering those in a different context, some Masons would connect that "outside" occurrence with Freemasonry. Most of the outlandish theories regarding the origins of Craft symbolism can be explained simply by lack of knowledge and education.

It is worth noting that in this mental process of assuming a connection, there is also a danger of reversing the time flow. Here is an extreme example to illustrate this. The graphic sign known as swastika was the emblem of the National Socialist (a.k.a. Nazi) party in the 20th century. Then we discover the same sign being used in ancient Indian sources. Next, the ignorant viewer would "retro-project" and write a Masonic education paper stating that ancient inhabitants of India were "Nazis".

Since the removal of classical erudition from the general curriculum, every ancient symbol and notion (sometimes full mythological stories embedded in our ceremonies) are encountered for the first time in the lodge. Hence – goes the logical fallacy – they were invented by Masons, and everybody else took them from us. Or had been a predecessor of Freemasonry.

The obvious explanation is two-fold: on the one hand ideas expressed with symbols are universal and present across cultures, and on the other hand, every new organization reaches left and right at their inception, freely borrowing stories, visible signs, ideas… Call it "cultural appropriation" if you will (to use a contemporary monster notion) but the cultural influences and interference are part of our reality since the dawn of mankind. And one last thing: if our own group, be it Masonry or any other organization, took a symbol or a narrative from a different source and moulded it for its needs, it doesn't make our group "lesser". Nothing to be ashamed of because we didn't invent the wheel… Instead, as an institution which has on its banners the idea of universality, we should proudly accept this cultural richness.

46 FAVOURITE SEVEN AT THE FESTIVE BOARD

You all have seen those playful questions "Who would you have dinner with?" or "Who are your favourite three or five or seven historical figures?" In this part you can read briefly about seven favourite Masons on my historical timeless list. I would like to sit with them in the lodge – to experience the many different rituals, and at the festive board (some call it harmony or agape) for a more informal chat during our meal.

Ivan VIII. Drašković Trakošćanski (1740 — 1787), a.k.a. Count Ivan *Drashkovich* (this would be the closest correct pronunciation). Croatian aristocrat, army officer in the Habsburg Empire, founder of his own Grand Lodge and Masonic system across the vast Empire that stretched from northern Italy to western Ukraine, and from Czechia to Croatia and Hungary with everything in between, including the author's homeland. They wrote all their documents in Latin: the constitution, the ritual, the minutes... I would have so many questions to ask! The ceremony of his initiation in a French lodge while being a prisoner of war in the Seven Years War. The decision to comprise seven degrees into three. The men he initiated into the Craft as his regiment was stationed in different towns of the Empire. His personal life and his favourite readings…

Angelo Soliman (?1721-1796). On a cold November day in 1796(!) a **Black man** had a stroke and collapsed on the street in Vienna. He died instantly. His body was taken home where a sculptor made a plaster cast of his upper body immediately. The next day, they took the corpse to a barn in the Burg and skinned it. Literally… and applied the skin to the wooden statue made by that sculptor. It was displayed with other Black men, and exotic animals in the Imperial Court Natural History Collection – until 1848, when the museum burned down during the revolutionary battles. This man, Angelo, was born in Africa, sold as a slave in his childhood and became one of the most educated people in Vienna, serving different aristocrats, and being a friend of the future emperor. He spoke many languages and studied history. From 1781 he was a member of famous and elite Viennese Masonic lodges. He must have known everyone who was important in the Austrian Enlightenment, so it would be difficult to decide what to ask him. About Francis I, the husband of Maria Theresa and later Holy Roman Emperor, or about Mozart or Haydn, or his travel – in his youth – to my homeland… Or the inevitable question: being a "Moor", a *blackamoor* in a white imperial city, and being treated even by his Masonic brothers as a strange curiosity of "nature"… [Even if time travel was possible, probably we shouldn't tell him that he was skinned after his death with the active participation of some Masons.]

Ignaz von Born (1742-1791) – A renowned expert in mineralogy, mining, and metallurgy, the founder of the *Kaiserliches Hofnaturalienkabinett* (Imperial Court Natural

History Collection, the forerunner of today's Weltmuseum Wien) where his friend, Angelo, later became an exhibit. Born is the only one in my list, who was born in my homeland, which makes him some kind of compatriot. His expertise in mining got him an invitation from Catherine the Great to supervise the Russian mines, but due to health reasons, he declined it. He was only seven years old when the first lodge in Transylvania was established, but later he probably knew many brothers from our homeland – a significant number of them were made Masons in Vienna. Most importantly, I would like to ask him about his plans to transform his lodge "Zur wahren Eintracht" into a potential "academy of science", an *Übungsloge* as they called it, a lodge of instruction, where the members presented papers which were discussed, and published in their Masonic Journal. It would be great to know how they did it. His help would be beneficial today in many of our lodges!

William Mercer Wilson (1813-1875), the first Grand Master of the independent Grand Lodge of Canada. Like so many of his contemporaries who became public figures, he studied law and had a career in that field. He was Grand Master multiple times, during difficult years of having a rival grand lodge in the West, and also during the division of the initial "Canada" grand lodge into two distinct bodies, as Québec went its own way[35]. I would have many important questions – if he would answer them (in his annual reports he chose not to reveal important issues). Both England and Scotland (from where our lodges originated) allow their lodges to use different rituals of

---

[35] Initially, the first Grand Lodge had jurisdiction in both Upper Canada (today's Ontario) and Lower Canada (Quebec). When Quebec formed its own Grand Lodge in 1869, it caused controversies, even with the name, so in 1887 the Masonic body in Ontario was renamed "Grand Lodge of Canada in the Province of Ontario".

their choice, so why is it that he rigidly insisted during the first annual communication (1856) to set up a committee to pick a *single* ritual to be adopted for the new jurisdiction? And the next year, in his address he alluded to some "theological" changes – innovations? – *forms and phrases*[36] introduced in the ritual to which some brothers objected. Rightly so, said the grand master. But what were those offending innovations? Why didn't he want to disclose them[37] and what did he decide to do about it? Finally, why didn't they have French-speaking lodges for those in Québec? Also, would he approve the state of Freemasonry today in his great jurisdiction?

---

[36] "Proceedings: Grand Lodge of A.F. and A.M. of Canada,1857 : Internet Archive." Internet Archive, https://archive.org/details/grandlodge1857onta p.174.

[37] Quote from the Address: "Objections had been raised by some highly esteemed brethren to the introduction of certain forms and phrases into our ritual, which conflicted with their religious belief and opinions; *it is unnecessary for me here to particularize either the forms or phrases* to which the brethren objected; but I feel it to be my duty distinctly to declare, that in my opinion these brethren had good grounds for their complaint; for as I understand Masonry—it is a Society to which men of all religions, moving within the pale of civilized society, who acknowledge the moral laws which bind the human family in the preservation of the social compact, and who admit a belief in the superintendence of a Deity over the universe which he has created, may be admitted and enrolled as members of its mystic fraternity; or, as it has been well defined by a distinguished brother, when he said :—'Free Masonry is an institution which welcomes equally to its bosom, the Jew and the Gentile, the Christian and Mahomedan, requiring from each only a just sense of moral rectitude and conscientious obligation.' If these definitions are correct, and I firmly believe them to be so, then the objections raised by the brethren referred to, are sustained, and the practice complained of, is pronounced an innovation and an excresence on the body of Masonry, which can neither be sanctioned, nor permitted."[*emphasis added*]

Joannovics György (1821-1909) & **Pulszky Ferenc** (1814-1897), with their name in the "correct" order: surname (last name) followed by Christian (first) name. Both were Grand Masters although that's not quite so simple. One was the first Grand Master of the English-style St John Grand Lodge, while the other presided in the Hungarian Grand Orient, working in the Scottish Rite tradition, following the French orientation. My questions would be about the "union" – the event that took place in 1886, and created one single Masonic body, uniting both the English (blue) lodges and French (red) lodges. Tell me about the backroom deals, please! How did you agree about the ritual (which was misnamed even at the time of my initiation there)? Why didn't they keep the more colourful and more interesting AASR[38] ritual? Do they know who contributed to the creation of Masonic vocabulary in our language? Can they help today to unite the Grand Lodge and the Grand Orient again?

Janovics Jenő (1872-1945), theatre director in my hometown in both meanings of the word: manager and directing productions. As a pioneer of the film industry in Eastern Europe he made over 60 movies from 1913 to 1920, having a studio on the shore of the small river where his "summer theatre" used to be. He was a successful director and actor, who also invited young talents and supported the launch of their careers. Two names stand out: Kertész Mihály (*Michael Curtiz* of Casablanca fame) and Korda Sándor (*Sir Alexander Korda*). His film enterprise was very profitable, but he spent all his personal wealth to finance the Hungarian theatre in my hometown, which he considered his real home, despite being born in

---

[38] AASR = Ancient & Accepted Scottish Rite. Despite the popular belief, it has beautiful rituals for the 1-3 degrees.

Uzhgorod[39]. When we sit down first of all I'd like to apologize for what Hungary did to him: as a Jew he had to hide underground during WWII, and even before that he was neglected for years. Next, I would want to hear about his lodge, *Unio*, where all the luminaries of the era were members including famous writers who were in our manuals when I went to school. What kind of lectures – *pieces of architecture*[40] – were presented by them in that lodge? Details about setting up a new lodge in Northern Transylvania? How did the lodge survive under different regimes? And, if it wasn't taboo, I would dare to ask him also about the beautiful actresses of his time…

Who would be your dinner guests?

---

[39] Uzhgorod (called Ungvár in Hungarian) – today a city in Ukraine. Janovics is buried in Kolozsvár, where he died on the stage of his beloved theatre.

[40] In many places, following the tradition of using the vocabulary of the operative Masons, the lectures presented in open lodge are called "pieces of architecture".

47 INHERITING THE HERITAGE

The idea that "old" buildings are part of our heritage and should be preserved is a relatively new idea. Consider that in the province of our jurisdiction (Ontario) such legislation aiming to protect our built heritage as monuments of the past was introduced only in 1975. The concept of preservation and restoration of old buildings became prominent worldwide in the second half of the 19th century.

In earlier times, people just added additional parts to the old structures, or built upon them, using parts of the old building, or they simply tore them down to build something new. If the structure was useful – like an aqueduct – they kept it because it served their interests. Other times they just re-used *the building stones* of the previous edifice and built something completely different. Back in my homeland, it was normal to learn about an 18th century castle that was built using some old stones from the nearby 11-12th century abandoned fortress. Or that a 16th century fortified castle became a prison, first in the dual Monarchy, and later, the same prison was used by the terrible communist regime for political prisoners, with upgraded security.

István Horváth

Then, in the late 20th century, the world developed this notion to keep intact old historical buildings, allegedly to preserve our history through conserving the built heritage. It sounds like a noble idea. Less for people living in a place that was categorized as a "heritage building"—which comes with tonnes of restrictions if the owner needs to renovate it.

But in today's contemplation, I wanted to talk about our **ritual(s)**. Diligent students familiar with the development of the different rituals between the 17th and 19th centuries, are aware that those ceremonies changed with time, some elements were forgotten, new—more contemporary—ideas and parts were added, just as it happened with those old-old buildings before we started to think of preserving them. Even with the buildings, many people feel that the reason behind this approach has never been explained clearly.

In the 1700s and 1800s a plethora of different rituals were born, most of the time using the basic elements (*building stones?*) of the originals – if there ever was an arch-ritual serving as the source for the variants to come – but often just creating something new instead of the inherited ceremony. Take, for example, the very popular Ancient and Accepted Scottish Rite ritual with its 33 degrees, and a specific ritual for each of them. Now, to put it bluntly, it is not "Scottish" and it is not "Ancient" either: we know exactly when it originated, and where, in France, to arrive to America through the Caribbean islands. And even on this continent, it just developed into a Southern, a Northern, and a Canadian version. In the first two hundred years of institutionalized Anglo-American Masonry, the ritual was re-written, edited, changed and – most importantly – adapted to the demands of the times. This is probably the most important lesson in today's chapter: adaptation to the changing times. Rituals were like living organisms: being created, growing, changing, adapting, sometimes even "dying", or just simply going out of vogue.

We need to ask, what happened about a hundred years ago, in the first half of the 20th century? Because most scholars point to that period, asserting that our heritage stopped being a living thing; from a flexible, adaptive idea, it became a rigid, inflexible bureaucratic institution. From that point, Freemasonry wasn't out there to serve men, but men had to be of service (servants?) to the institution. The roles got reversed.

Yes, the magnificent virtual edifice erected by our Masonic ancestors is still there as we inherited it, but exactly as with the heritage buildings, we cannot rebuild or adapt it to our needs, because our own internal regulations don't allow it. We handcuffed ourselves inside this beautiful imaginary edifice, which is Freemasonry, and locked ourselves in… and now we are waiting for someone to liberate us. But the world doesn't even know that we are there!

What would you change in your ritual?

48 THE TEMPLARS: LEGENDS AND MORE LEGENDS

I discovered the Templar's story before I met the first Mason in my life. A French author, journalist, and traveller wrote a book about the Templar "mysteries" before the topic became so popular in Western culture (Charpentier, *Les mystères templiers.*)[41] There were vague mentions of the knights during my history classes since they owned fortifications and villages in the medieval Hungarian Kingdom, but students don't pay attention to such boring details.

Then came Charpentier and his book, almost like a revelation. Not because of fanciful conspiracy theories or outlandish claims of non existing connections, but because of the cultural contributions of the order during its existence. Their early "banking system" is well known by now, but they also brought innovations in architecture, agriculture, and other economic domains – according to this author. This was the book from which I learned about

---

[41] Charpentier, Louis. *Les mystères templiers.* Les énigmes de l'univers. Paris: Robert Laffont, 1967.

their legendary naval fleet at La Rochelle, which completely disappeared when the order was dismantled. Where did they go? (Usually, here comes the "*La Merika*" debate[42]...)

Without exaggerating the objectivity or historical value of the book, it made me fall in love with the "poor soldiers of Christ", as their full name[43] was, and their legendary story also inspired me to read many other books dealing with the history of medieval world. There was no Google at the time and even the accessible web (especially in Eastern Europe) was of no particular help. But we had books and libraries, and the old methods of research I learned at the university as a hopeful future philologist: notes, cards and more cards, and more books, and more notes. It is boring for any outsider, and even with the improved – or at least easier to handle – digital versions, the process is still the same. Get inspired and elaborate a theory or hypothesis, start working on it, and find literature (scholarly books, journal articles, essays, studies, but not fictional works) that could and would support your idea. As simple as it sounds, most of the time it is completely ignored by the self-appointed "experts" in the Masonic discussion groups.

The discussion goes in this manner: Person A – The tooth fairy is real. We know that and there are many books about her. Person B – No, she is not, she's an imaginary figure in the folklore. Person A – Prove it!

Here is the problem: with those boring methods mentioned above, we also learned that the onus of providing proof is on the proponent of the new theory or idea! For the opponents, it is enough to dismiss it as an

---

[42] There is a popular belief that the fleet sailed toward west, following a star named La Merika, and from the wrong French spelling of it as *L'America* the new continent got its name.
[43] The Poor Fellow-Soldiers of Christ and of the Temple of Solomon (Latin: *Pauperes commilitones Christi Templique Salomonici*)

unproven theory. Let's say I would love to find a connection between the Templar Knights and the Masonic lodges. But there is a few centuries "gap" in time between the two groups. For fictional bestsellers, that's not a problem: their authors always can invent a "hidden" history. Actually, that is exactly the job of such novels and movie stories: to present an *invented* story to entertain their readers and viewers[44]. However, in a scholarly essay or book one must bring irrefutable proof based on sources that can be checked by others as well.

Obviously, there is a difference between an exchange of ideas and polemics in a reputable scholarly journal and a casual discussion in an online forum. Without denying that, we should stick to the basic lessons of logic, even in our more casual talks. Masonic discourse often refers to the seven liberal arts and sciences, and Logic is one of those.

If we don't apply the "art" in our everyday life, why do we bother talking about it?

P.S. I still love the exciting Templar stories, I just don't have proof for their underground survival in the guilds…

---

[44] Dictionary definitions for "fiction": a) literature in the form of prose that describes imaginary events and people; b) the type of book or story that is written about imaginary characters and events and not based on real people and facts.

49 BARN RAISING OR BAR RAISING

Which one describes better our North American Freemasonry? If the question doesn't make sense at first sight, consider this.

The other day I was mentioning in a casual discussion the Hungarian notion of "kaláka". The Romanians call it "clacă", the former Yugoslavs say "moba" - and for years I tried to figure out the English word for it. As it turned out, the activity is not unknown, but lacking a simple word, there is a phrase for it – *"barn raising"*. When a community comes together to help one of their own with a task that is too big for one family. A **ritualized form of community service** and participation, which recalls sweet memories from the Transylvanian village where I spent my summers as a child, and seemingly unrelated to Masonic topics.

When I became affiliated with my "stepmother lodge" in Canada, I knew little about barn raising or the peculiarities of the *style of Masonry* that is practiced on this continent, to use an expression borrowed from a distinguished Masonic author[45]. The "style" of North

---

[45] Jackson, Thomas William. *North American Freemasonry: Idealism and Realism*. Washington, DC: Plumbstone, 2019.

István Horváth

American Masonry was defined as charitable, focused on community service – or raising the barn if we think in the terms of the "kaláka". That's where the dilemma formulated in the title above becomes relevant to the present discussion. Although many active Masons don't perceive it in those terms, simply because we rarely analyze what seems to be our natural world. We live in it, and we don't think about it.

If not the barn, then what is that *"bar"* which we are supposed to raise? Some might say it is the same as guarding the West Gate. On other continents, they consider it "raising the bar" as being very selective when accepting new members. *Raising the bar* in that context is alluding to the quality of men whom they admit to the Craft. In many places, there is constant care to attract the best and the brightest men into the lodges. Often, in North America, this is considered elitist (and there is a separate article in this book dedicated to this controversy), although it is difficult to find a comprehensive definition of the term. Sometimes it seems to be like in the joke: if I can't join this club then it means they are too elitist…

And this might also raise another controversy in our Masonic philosophy. We claim rightly that the lodges functioned as the incubators of the budding democracy at the dawn of the Enlightenment era. And with democratic systems, we associate equal rights, equal opportunities, and the participation of the *demos* (people) in the affairs of the society. So, how can we reconcile those concepts with the selectiveness of certain jurisdictions, where the applicants are placed on year-long waiting lists, and are subject to a rigorous vetting process? Maybe there is a simple explanation to it. People often think of "democratic" institutions or groups as wide open to everyone, allowing mass participation.

But what if Freemasonry was never intended to be a "mass organization"? Or was it? Could this be another case of confronting *idealism and realism*?

50 LODGES AND LODGES

What is the lodge? Many people associate it with our buildings. In the 20th century when the fraternity had a huge membership, labour was cheap (at least considerably cheaper than today), and big undertakings were the order of the day – lodges and grand lodges started erecting big and mostly beautiful buildings, which were, according to one Masonic scholar, always in the centre of cities, towns, next to the town hall, the church, the courthouse – and maybe the pub. An integral part of the city's infrastructure.

By today, these building are in most cases impossible to maintain, the upkeep costs are enormous, and the dwindling membership is not able – and not willing, even if they deny it – to maintain them. And these buildings are practically useless because most of the days they are empty.

One issue is not the decreasing number of members but the unwillingness to *increase the dues*. Historically, when those magnificent edifices were erected, the average dues were a much higher percentage of the members' income. We often complain about the erosion by inflation of our net income, however, Masons are reluctant to even consider how inflation is affecting their never-increasing dues. Present dues are worthless in many places, when contrasted with the ongoing expenses of a lodge. A hundred years ago, the average annual dues were equal to one week's income. One can only imagine the outrage if someone would dare to make such a suggestion…

Another answer to the initial question would be that the lodge is the *group of people*, the group of Masons united in a specific form of assembly, sanctioned by the grand lodge of the land. From this perspective, ownership of a building is more a burden than a joy. Many lodges of Masons are so caught up in maintenance issues (property taxes, insurance, utilities, renovations etc.) that their whole Masonic life revolves around managing the building… forgetting almost everything about real Freemasonry.

I had the chance to visit a few world-famous Masonic buildings as well as small rural lodges in the Prairies, and many others in between. While the huge ornate buildings are awe-inspiring by their proportions and exquisite decorations, my personal preference is towards the small lodge rooms. A **small lodge room** is easier to be filled with members to create the impression that it is full of people. In a large room, even the same number of members present would give you that unpleasant feeling of emptiness and disinterest.

No, small lodge rooms will not improve Masonry by themselves. However, they could create a better starting point for the Masonic experience. They radiate warmth and create energy.

So, what should we preserve? The buildings or the people?

Disclosure. None of my lodges owns a building.

51 MYSTERY PLAYS AND THE HIRAMIC LEGEND

Isn't that some kind of medieval churchy thing? Biblical scenes played for the illiterate masses in and around the churches? Some kind of drama that later was banned in Elizabethan England? – All that is true. But there is more to it. Interestingly, in Eastern Europe, notably in Poland and Hungary, rural mystery plays are still a living tradition: as they call it in folklore, "peasant mystery plays" are still performed.

A few years ago, in some parts of England, for example, in the city of York, the medieval mystery plays tradition was revived, and the Guild of Builders(!) presented *The Creation*[46].

Let's step back, or maybe forward in time, from the medieval era to the early 1700s, and contemplate the three basic degrees of Freemasonry.

Everybody knows or should know that the third degree was a late addition, after the creation of the "premier"

---

[46] See their YouTube channel:
https://www.youtube.com/playlist?list=PLLcNhwT70KSgeDsSlCj4NOxs3lcrycDTs (accessed 2023-07-13)

Grand Lodge of London and Westminster in 1717.

Even if we had no records, just by looking at the structure of the ceremony, it should be obvious that the three degrees are different: the Entered Apprentice (EA) and the Fellow Craft (FC) degrees can be regarded as a two-stage initiation with abundant moral (or if you are more critical: moralistic) teachings, e.g. don't screw your master's wife – *"[...]that he covet not the wife, not the daughter, of his masters, neither of his fellows, but if it be in marriage, nor hold concubines, for discord that might fall amongst them.'*[47] Of course, it conveys more important things as well, instructing the candidate to follow the moral code of conduct (EA), and to study the laws of nature (FC).

In how they are built and how the sequences of action and "parts" (text) follow each other, the first two degrees are very similar: they follow a pattern well known by cultural anthropologists under the term rites of passage. Just a reminder: at the beginning there were only these two degrees. But the third one, which was added to the ritual during the 1720s, is modelled after a different pattern.

There the candidate becomes the protagonist of a drama. The ritual is not only an "illustration", but it requires that the candidate actively partake in it, as the main character, Hiram Abiff. It is full of archaic elements conveying evergreen philosophical talking points: death, honour, loyalty, human greed, crime, and punishment. It is known as the *Hiramic legend*. Minor problem: it has nothing to do with the character with the same name from the Bible (1 Kings 7:12-14; 2 Chronicles 2:13-14) – It is an invented story portraying a fictional character, yet it became crucial (maybe the wrong word here for a dead

---

[47] Speth, George William. *Quatuor Coronatorum Antigrapha*. Masonic Reprints ... Edited by G.W. Speth. N.p., "Keble's Gazette" Office, 1889. It contains the Cooke MS, from where the quote originates.

and raised person[48]) in the Craft ceremony.

Where did the legend come from? Who "inserted" it into the ritual, creating a formerly nonexistent grade? That's where we may want to return to the medieval mystery plays. Although, it has to be said: no mystery play ever had as the main or minor character said brass worker, Hiram from Tyre (not the King of Tyre).

Regarding the origins, theories abound. In the Transactions of the Lodge of Research No. 2429, Leicester (England) for the Year 1903-1904, the author listed 14 different hypotheses at that time[49]… A significant addition to that list in the next one hundred years was the consideration given to the mystery plays. Any Mason following this path must understand that we are not talking about the content of any peculiar mystery play, but about the structure, the drama. The American (Preston-Webb) ritual has even more dramatic elements than the Canadian Work based on Emulation: that ritual preserved a pre-Union variant, closer to the Antient Grand Lodge ritual.

Now we know that for centuries, different guilds and incorporations had been in charge of certain plays that they had to finance and perform on the occasions established by the city and the local church. It is not very farfetched to think that the dramatic form of mystery plays might have influenced the form and structure of the third degree[50].

However, lately the most accepted theory suggests that it was written and added by John Th. Desaguliers, and given his French family background some refer rather to a

---

[48] Allusion to the ideas that identify Hiram Abiff as representing Jesus Christ of the New Testament.
[49] Hextall, W.B. *The Hiramic Legend and the Ashmolean Theory*: Foundations of Freemasonry Series (p. 6). Lamp of Trismegistus. Kindle Edition.
[50] Davis, Robert G. The Mason's Words: The History and Evolution of the American Masonic Ritual. 2013. pp. 89-96

Chanson de Geste, a medieval type of French legend.[51]

Considering that even in earlier documents, i.e. before the 1720s when the degree was added, the Hiramic legend was mentioned (by scarce references), we cannot discard the influence of mystery plays, acting as templates for the new additional degree. It also took over part of the former Fellow Craft degree, as is proven by unexpected references to the second degree in the text. Also worth noting is that the part of the installation of the Master of the Lodge (which used to be the only "master" prior to the third grade) is conducted in the Fellow Craft degree.

Desaguliers might be the most likely person to be behind this early "innovation", but his sources are unknown, and we can just guess about them.

Personally, I am inclined to give credit to those theories that look at the mystery plays.

What is your pick?

---

[51] Powell, Christopher. "The Hiramic Legend and the Creation of the Third Degree." *AQC*, vol. 134, 2021, pp. 65–113.

52 WHAT ABOUT YOUR SOUL?

In a considerable number of jurisdictions, among them even in a few liberally inclined ones, besides the belief in a Supreme Being, a strange question is asked which has very peculiar religious ramifications.

The question asked refers to the *immortality of the soul*. And the candidate has to have an opinion about it, and "confess" his thoughts as an answer to the question. Or just say a simple yes or no. For people who were brought up in certain religions and denominations, the entire issue is not a big deal.

For others, however, it could be. And that is always the problem with religious questions thrown onto the application forms, perhaps by people lacking any kind of theological education or insight. And it happens in any organization that succeeds in escaping vigilant secularist censors.

As always, in Western culture, we need to go back to antiquity, to the Old Greeks, and meet Plato to find the origins of this question. Theologians agree that there is no reference to an immortal soul in the Old Testament. Of course, in far more ancient teachings and religions, such as Indian philosophy and religion, the idea of reincarnation involves the immortality of the soul. Should we say it revolves around it?

We could write a book presenting the history of the idea, and debating with the different philosophers and theologians of bygone eras to find an answer that would settle the issue for all Masons. The question is: can the question be answered in such a way that satisfies all Masons of all religious persuasions?

With topics of a religious character, beyond the personal creed and conviction, there is a more general, a more philosophical aspect to the question. Cultural anthropologists stated that some kind of belief in an afterlife was already present in mankind's ancient history, in what we call pre-history, for example in the veneration of fallen warrior heroes. Then, from Plato to medieval Christianity, and from Blaise Pascal to Kant and to present theologians and philosophers, many great minds attempted to resolve the issue once and for all.

In some religious traditions, however, the afterlife became a reward of a moral life, lived according to the tenets of that religion. In darker periods of human history, we have documented cases when representatives of a religious dogma forced groups of conquered populations to adhere to beliefs and moral codes in order "to save their souls".

And here comes the complication: if one believes in the immortality of the soul in general, then it means that every man's souls is immortal. If so, is there really a need for "saving" them? Or do we have again an Orwellian case where some souls are more immortal than others?

Philosophical question: can a man who doesn't believe in the immortality of the soul still choose the good and not because he's hoping for a reward in the afterlife but because the morally good should be the option in itself? If the answer is yes, why is the belief in immortality considered superior?

Most people would have difficulties even with the definition of the soul.

An interesting private project suggestion for the readers could be finding out what kind of questions are asked to the candidate in other jurisdictions. You may be surprised…

EPILOGUE (BONUS CHAPTER)

After so much "criticism" and "doubts" maybe I should offer a more positive conclusion to dispel the impression that I am an unhappy Freemason. True, I am occasionally disappointed by events or people or mainly the general lack of intellectual challenges in the lodges. During the years, though, I learned to focus on things that bring joy and fulfilment, restoring my hope in the future of Freemasonry.

First was the discovery of the *Masonic Restoration Foundation* (and now I am trying to be a regular attendant at their Annual Symposium) opening my eyes to the Observant movement. Then came the young Masons and their willingness to learn and immerse in the deeper meanings of the Craft. When I compiled a small presentation delineating my vision for the post-pandemic Freemasonry and another one for a virtual time capsule, I had in mind the next generations.

The Observant movement was a revelation in my Masonic journey on this continent: after my visit to Ontario's first Observant lodge, *Templum Fidelis*, I was sure I would like to be part of such a group. I was lucky because soon after I wrote about it enthusiastically, a brother invited me to participate in forming an Observant lodge. I had no idea at that time that the brother would soon be our Grand Master and later the author of the *Foreword* to this volume. Ever since then I am a proud member of *Templum Lucis* (The Temple of the Light), and I was honoured by my brethren to be appointed several times as their speaker. Our lodge meetings always feature two speakers, one in the lodge and another one at the formal festive board.

Having a lecture, a *piece of architecture*, as it was called in my mother lodge in Europe, gives me the familiar feeling of learning and widening our horizons, something I used to experience at the beginning of my journey. Beyond that, I enjoy the entire experience, as the lodge setting is appealing to (almost) all our senses: music, and a contemplation period after it, candles to create that play of light and shadow (darkness) to mesmerize the participants, the fascinating guest speakers to stimulate our minds, and the elegant catered dining with more stimulating ideas. Some sister lodges of the Observant movement use even incense, and that adds another dimension to it. And the Chain of the Union, performed after the ritualistic closing, enforces that feeling of *unhesitating cordiality*.

If I have to describe succinctly why I need to be in an Observant lodge: *to experience meeting with like-minded men*! (Some say observant lodges are not for everyone. True. Just as Freemasonry is not for everyone, even if we often forget about it, trying—in vain—to be too inclusive.) I will not apologize for supporting wholeheartedly the Observant movement and its ideals, although I know that some conformist long-time Masons discard it too easily as "elitist", because they want everything in their old ways.

But our future is in the hands of the *next generations* coming behind us. I truly believe their commitment to the initial ideals of Freemasonry and their interest in creating a more meaningful lodge experience for themselves might be what will save the Craft from the boredom established as the norm by my generation. When I look at the officers' line in my "stepmother" lodge, and see young Master Masons eager to shape the future of it, I root for them. And I had them in my mind when I summarized my expectations for the "post-pandemic" Freemasonry. Here is the short version of that list:

Difficult to join. Make it a *privilege*.

Be a **unique, exclusive** group of likeminded men.

Have only highly **qualified likeminded** men.

Put high **value** on the unique experience! Don't sell it cheap.

Investigators **must judge** the character.

No more degree **mills**…

If necessary, **lose a few** members (*separate the chaff from the wheat*)

Raise the dues to cover your expenses!

Have **small** lodges.

Mentoring by levels: *literary, allegorical, symbolic*.

Get rid of the "progression line" for officers – **by merit only**.

Rethink and reform the Grand Lodge **evaluation** criteria!

Each item on that list deserves a separate discussion, as I presented in many lodges where I was invited to talk. (An elaborate version is also available on my blog.) I enjoyed the feedback even if many older Masons didn't agree with those ideas. They don't have to, as long as the younger brothers have the courage to fight the conformism and ignorance.

In a more international context, when VOOSA called their speakers and presenters to give a brief talk for a virtual time capsule during their 100th meeting, we all looked forward to the next one hundred years to envision the unimaginable: *big sweeping changes and reforms*.

The following were the ideas I presented there: a new approach to the *universal* brotherhood we preach so much about—hypocritically, to be honest… I am embarrassed when after exposing the noble ideas of the fraternity, I have to admit that we exclude a quarter of the world's Freemasons because of their tolerance and creed (or lack of), and another big group because of their skin colour, not to mention half of the population because of their gender. Make no mistake: I like and want to keep my male-only lodge and organization. Just feel ashamed when some Masons display unreasonable hatred toward women or atheist Masons that teach the same spiritual and moral values in their own organization...

Furthermore, let's end the colonial English paternalism toward the rest of the world. No Grand Lodge, including UGLE, should be in charge to define Masonry for others. The present worldwide structure is anachronistic and outdated!

All bodies should be in amicable relations: the Grand Lodges, the Grand Orients, the Valleys, the Chapters, and the head honchos of the future!

That's what I envision for the future: a more inclusive mentality which does not exclude maintaining the specifics of each lodge and each Grand Lodge—but *without the dogmatism* of the present system. (It is a medieval religious inheritance to think that everything that is not exactly as my belief must be heretic.)

Without such a fundamental change, which could differ from my vision, but it's inevitable, Freemasonry will die out.

I wish the next generations to be smarter and wiser than we were...

About the author

A Mason on two continents and in different languages, István Horváth started his Masonic journey late: only after the collapse of the Berlin Wall, when Freemasonry became legal in the former Eastern Bloc in Europe. Before moving to Canada, where he's settled now in Hamilton, Ontario, he worked as a journalist, and a few years ago he started to write and present lectures about the Craft in English. The COVID years became more prolific than any other time, so he received invitations from many local and international groups and Masonic bodies to present papers researched and written during this period. He is a member of several Masonic research lodges and societies. Besides his keen interest in the Craft, he also blogs in English and Hungarian about public affairs. This is his first book written and published in English.

  https://masonicfootnotes.com
  https://twitter.com/OtherMason
  https://www.facebook.com/IstvanHorvathAuthor/

BIBLIOGRAPHY

Works cited or recommended

"Proceedings: Grand Lodge of A.F. and A.M. of Canada,1857 : Grand Lodge : Free Download, Borrow, and Streaming: Internet Archive." *Internet Archive*, archive.org/details/grandlodge1857onta.

Barker, Kenneth L., and Donald W. Burdick. *The NIV Study Bible*. 10th anniversary ed. Grand Rapids, MI: Zondervan Pub. House, 1995.

Berman, Ric. *Foundations of Modern Freemasonry: The Grand Architects — Political Change and the Scientific Enlightenment, 1714 -1740*. 2011. *Bowker*.

Berman, Ric. *Schism*. Liverpool University Press, 2013.

Camp, Pannill. "The Stage Art of Brotherhood: Sentimental Dramaturgy and Mid-Century Franc-Maçonnerie." *Philological Quarterly* (2014): Vol. 93, Iss. 1: 117-138. Iowa City.

Camp, Pannill. "The Theatrical Beauty of Initiation Ritual." *California Freemason*, vol. 64, no. 4, Apr. 2016, pp. 3–6.

Cirlot, Juan-Eduardo C. *A Dictionary of Symbols*, 1972. https://doi.org/10.1604/9780802220837.

Coil, Henry W. *A Comprehensive View of Freemasonry*, 2002. https://doi.org/10.1604/9780880530538.

Comenius, Johann Amos. *Pansophiae Prodromus: Et Conatuum Pansophicorum Dilvcidatio: Accedent Didactica Dissrtatio de Sfrnuonis Latini Studie Perfecte Abplvendo, Aliaqve Eivsdem by Johann Amos Comenius - Books on Google Play*. https://play.google.com/store/books/details?id=Wg9CA AAAcAAJ&rdid=book-Wg9CAAAAcAAJ&rdot=1. Accessed 17 July 2023.

Comenius, Johann Amos. *Via lucis vestigata et vestiganda, hoc est Rationabilis disquisitio, quibus modis intellectualis animorum lux, Sapientia, per omnes omnium hominum mentes et gentes jam tandem sub mundi vesperam feliciter spargi possit. Libellus ante annos viginti sex in Anglia scriptus, nunc demum typis exscriptus et in Angliam remissus.* [The Way of the Light followed and appropriate for following, that is, a Rational discourse, which might finally and happily diffuse into the minds of all people and nations the intellectual light of the Spirit, Wisdom, before the twilight of the world. A book written in England twenty-six years ago, now in print for the first time and sent back to England.] Amsterdam. 1668.

D. Cooper, Robert L. *Cracking the Freemasons Code: The Truth about Solomon's Key and the Brotherhood.* Beyond Words/Atria Books, 2007. https://doi.org/10.1604/9781416546825.

Cooper, Robert L.D. *The Rosslyn Hoax?*, 2007.

Davis, Robert G. *The Mason's Words: The History and Evolution of the American Masonic Ritual.* 2013. Bowker.

Gandoff, Martin. *Over 300 Years of Masonic Ritual*, 2017.

Hammer, Andrew. *Observing the Craft.* Mindhive Books, 2015.

Harland-Jacobs, Jessica L. *Builders of Empire: Freemasons and British Imperialism, 1717-1927*, 2007. https://doi.org/10.1604/9780807830888.

Harrison, David. *The Lost Rites and Rituals of Freemasonry*, 2017.

Hoyos, Arturo, and Stephen Morris. *The Perfect Ceremonies of Craft Masonry and the Holy Royal Arch*, 2021.

Hunt, Lynn, Margaret C. Jacob, and Wijnand Mijnhardt. *The Book That Changed Europe: Picart and Bernard's Religious Ceremonies of the World.* Belknap Press, 2010.

Jackson, Thomas W. *North American Freemasonry: Idealism and Realism*, 2019.

Jacob, Margaret C. *Living the Enlightenment: Freemasonry and Politics in Eighteenth-Century Europe*, 1991. https://doi.org/10.1604/9780195070514.

Jacob, Margaret C. *The Origins of Freemasonry: Facts and*, 2007. https://doi.org/10.1604/9780812219883.

Knoop, Douglas. *The Early Masonic Catechisms.* 1993. *Bowker*, doi:10.1604/9781564593245.

Meletinsky, Eleazar M. *Poetics of Myth*. Routledge, 2014. *Bowker*.

Murphy, Christopher B., and Shawn Eyer, eds. *Exploring Early Grand Lodge Freemasonry: Studies in Honor of the Tricentennial of the Establishment of the Grand Lodge of England*, 2017.

Nordquist, Richard. "Stylistics and Elements of Style in Literature." ThoughtCo, Aug. 26, 2020, thoughtco.com/stylistics-language-studies-1692000. (accessed September 28, 2022).

Önnerfors, Andreas J. "(PDF) Jan Snoek: RESEARCHING FREEMASONRY: WHERE ARE WE | Andreas J Önnerfors - Academia.Edu." *Academia.Edu - Share Research*, 1 Jan. 2008, https://www.academia.edu/43128946/Jan_Snoek_RESEARCHING_FREEMASONRY_WHERE_ARE_WE.

Önnerfors, Andreas. "Borders of historical hermeneutics: do we really understand performance?" *Unpublished paper.* (2008) https://www.academia.edu/39780539/BORDERS_OF_HISTORICAL_HERMENEUTICS_DO_WE_REALLY_UNDERSTAND_PERFORMANCE_ (accessed September 28, 2022)

Önnerfors, Andreas. *Freemasonry: A Very Short Introduction*. 2017. *Bowker*.

Péter, Róbert, "General Introduction" & "Bibliography" in R. Péter (general editor), C. Révauger (volume editor), *British Freemasonry, 1717-1813*, 5 vols. (New York: Routledge, 2016), vol. 1., p. xiv.

Péter, Róbert, editor. *British Freemasonry, 1717-1813*. Routledge, 2016. *Bowker*.

Péterfy, Gergely,. *Kitömött Barbár*. Kalligram, 2014.

Pike, Kenneth Lee, and Evelyn G. Pike. *Grammatical Analysis*. Publication in Linguistics 53. Dallas Arlington (Tex.): Summer Institute of linguistics the University of Texas, 1982.

"PS Review of Freemasonry." *PS Review of Freemasonry*,

http://www.freemasons-freemasonry.com.

Powell, Christopher. "The Hiramic Legend and the Creation of the Third Degree." *AQC*, vol. 134, 2021, pp. 65–113.

Roberts, Allen E., and Wallace McLeod. *Freemasonry and Democracy: Its Evolution in North America*. 1997. *Bowker*, doi:10.1604/9780935633184.

Roucek, Josef S. "Jan Amos Komenský: The Spiritual Founder of Modern Masonic Mouvement." *Zeitschrift Für Religions- Und Geistesgeschichte*, vol. 15, no. 4, Brill, pp. 371–76, doi:10.2307/23894786. Accessed 1 July 2023.

Snoek, Jan. "Researching Freemasonry: Where Are We?" *CRFF Working Paper Series* No. 2. (2008) https://www.academia.edu/43128946/Jan_Snoek_RESEARCHING_FREEMASONRY_WHERE_ARE_WE (accessed September 28, 2002).

Snoek. *Initiating Women in Freemasonry*. BRILL, 2012.

"The Constitutions of the Free-masons, Containing the History, Charges, Regulations, &C. Of That Most Ancient and Right Worshipful Fraternity. For the Use of the Lodges - Google Play." *The Constitutions of the Free-masons, Containing the History, Charges, Regulations, &C. Of That Most Ancient and Right Worshipful Fraternity. For the Use of the Lodges - Google Play Books*, play.google.com/books/reader?id=LkICAAAAQAAJ&pg=GBS.PP10.

Stevenson, David. *The Origins of Freemasonry: Scotland's Century, 1590-1710*, 2010. https://doi.org/http://dx.doi.org/10.1017/CBO9780511560828https://doi.org/10.1017/CBO9780511560828.

Wigger, Iris, and Spencer Hadley. "Angelo Soliman: Desecrated Bodies and the Spectre of Enlightenment Racism." *Race & Class*, vol. 62, no. 2, SAGE Publications, Aug. 2020, pp. 80–107. *Crossref*, doi:10.1177/0306396820942470.

www.ingramcontent.com/pod-product-compliance
Lightning Source LLC
Chambersburg PA
CBHW071711020426
42333CB00017B/2216